BITE BOOKS

A Bite-Sized Public Affairs Book

Whatever Happened to the Meritocracy?

Personal Stories of Growing Up in the '50s and '60s

Edited by

Margaret Peacock

Cover by
Dean Stockton

Published by Bite-Sized Books Ltd 2020
©Margaret Peacock 2020

BITE-SIZED BOOKS

Bite-Sized Books Ltd Cleeve Road, Goring RG8 9BJ UK
information@bite-sizedbooks.com

Registered in the UK. Company Registration

No: 9395379

ISBN: 9798552150014

The moral right of Margaret Peacock be identified as the author of this work has been asserted by her in accordance with the Copyright, Designs and Patents

Act 1988

Although the publisher, editors and authors have used reasonable care in preparing this book, the information it contains is distributed as is and without warranties of any kind. This book is not intended as legal, financial, social or technical advice and not all recommendations may be suitable for your situation. Professional advisors should be consulted as needed. Neither the publisher nor the author shall be liable for any costs, expenses or damages resulting from use of or reliance on the information contained in this book.

Contents

Foreword   2
  The Return of the Meritocracy Debate
    Sir Vince Cable
Editorial Note   6
The Contributors   12
Chapter 1   14
  Tambourines to Tolstoy
    Margaret Peacock
Chapter 2   35
  Continuing to Live
    Barry Simner
Chapter 3   57
  It's Still Home and They Are Home Truths
    Diana Milnes
Chapter 4   77
  The '60s Meritocracy – MINO
    Paul Davies
Bite-Sized Public Affairs Books   96
Bite-Sized Books Catalogue   97

Foreword

The Return of the Meritocracy Debate

Sir Vince Cable

It may seem a little odd to be worrying about meritocracy when Britain is on its second Etonian Prime Minister out of three, and not especially competent at that; when the United States has a President of questionable merit who became a wealthy man on the back of his father's fortune; and when, even in the new Superpower of Communist China, a dictatorial leader has emerged who was a 'princeling' of a privileged, well-connected, family.

Yet there is now an intellectual fashion to debunk the supposed triumph of the meritocrats. The fashion has been led by Michael Sandel, the moral and political philosopher. He built his international reputation questioning the ethical underpinnings of societies based on markets, where everything has a price. He has moved on in his latest book, *The Tyranny of Merit,* to argue that the polarised, poisonous, politics of today is a reaction against the way success is rewarded by wealth and acclamation in societies which are unequal and stratified. Those who are left behind in low paid and low status jobs, the failures, have nothing left to rescue their self-respect apart from their anger and resentment.

The belief that out society was becoming too deferential to 'merit' is far from new. Aldous Huxley's *Brave New World* was a satire about a world in which the clever Alphas had all the wealth and power and the failures, the stupid and the losers –the Epsilons- were allotted menial tasks serving their intelligent superiors. A more targeted criticism, from the sociologist Michael Young in *The Rise of the Meritocracy,* amongst others, was of emerging, post-war, Britain in which a society based on merit was being designed through selective schooling. The clever-clogs who passed the 11+ went off to Grammar schools and from there to university and the professions where they could rule over their dimmer contemporaries who failed this supposedly definitive test of intelligence and were condemned to Secondary Moderns and, then, manual, menial, work.

In the event, there was a popular revolt against the 11+. Faith in the IQ test was badly dented by evidence that it was a poor measure of potential ability, covering only a narrow aspect of cognitive skills, and could be improved with practice (I was one of those IQ stars-getting one of highest scores recorded in my city-having practised for months on test papers, supervised by my father). There was a reaction against children being divided into clever sheep and stupid goats. The 11+ disappeared in most parts of the country and Grammar schools became a rarity, to be replaced by Comprehensives. And within the Comprehensive sector there was a reaction against rewards and praise for success, academic or sporting, lest this should demotivate the losers.

But that reaction against meritocracy did little to make Britain a more equal and fairer place. The fee-paying independent sector, where attendance is primarily dependent upon parental wealth, survived and has flourished and its pupils dominate positions of power rather more than the grammar school boys and girls. And a new barrier was created at 16+ or 18+ when children from less privileged backgrounds were, in general, less equipped to progress through competitive examinations to leading universities and from there to success in many walks of life.

And that, in turn, raises the question of what is the alternative to advancement on merit when ability, variously defined, is rewarded materially and with respect. In practice, the alternative is not a happy, egalitarian, cooperative, relaxed paradise in which we all bestow mutual respect on all our fellow citizens. Would that it were. And where it happens, as fleetingly during the pandemic when we all clapped in appreciation of van drivers, supermarket packers, hospital porters and other 'essential' employees, there is a sense of a better world.

But the threat to the values of that better world don't primarily come from meritocracy but from those with a hereditary sense of entitlement. There is lot of evidence that in the UK and in the USA, amongst other countries, social mobility is slowing down. Social strata are becoming more rigid with fewer genuine 'rags to riches' stories and fewer underprivileged families seeing their offspring 'make it' to positions of power, influence, wealth and status. By contrast, 'to them that have shall be given'; inherited wealth and the advantages of being brought up in an educated family determine our life chances.

So, instead of attacking merit, what should be done? Should we praise or abuse Steve Jobs and Jeff Bezos for being multi-billionaires? We should praise their entrepreneurial ability but make sure that they pay proper taxes for the undoubted public sector help they received on the way up and fierce inheritance tax on their legacies (as Bill Gates has also argued). Should we praise or abuse the Oxbridge or Imperial College starred firsts who epitomise our ideals of scholastic merit. We should praise their achievement but expect them to pay back the costs of their subsidised university education and ensure that everyone from the next generation gets the 'early years' support so that they can compete on a level playing field.

I have to say that I am a lot more comfortable with other peoples' rewards for merit than with the entitlements of birth.

The enemies of merit need to be clear that they are not the friends of aristocratic privilege and caste.

About the Contributor

The Rt Hon Sir Vince Cable was Secretary of State for Business Innovation and Skills and President of the Board of Trade (2010-2015). He was Member of Parliament for Twickenham 1997-2015; deputy leader of the Lib Dems 2007-2010 and shadow chancellor 2003-2010.

He was the leader of the Liberal Democrats 2017-2019; he has served as Member of Parliament for Twickenham 1997-2015, 2017-2019.

Vince Cable read Natural Sciences and Economics at Cambridge University, where he was President of the Union, followed by a PhD at Glasgow University.

Vince served as a Labour councillor in Glasgow between 1971 and 1974, before joining the Social Democrat party. He is currently a visiting professor at the London School of Economics.

Editorial Introduction

Margaret Peacock

The idea for this book came to me when, like many others during the first Covid lockdown, I started to write my autobiography, not for publication, but for my children. It was writing about my experience of my 1950's grammar school which led me to reflect how those of us born soon after the war, now in our 70s, constituted the first wave of the meritocracy introduced by the 1944 Education Act, with its tripartite system. I thought that it might be interesting, therefore, in the light of what has happened in education in the seven decades since then, to ask some of my contemporaries to recollect their emotions and experiences of the time when the world started to change, and clever working class children were consciously drafted into the professions to support the growing post war economy.

The book would be a collection of short autobiographies, illustrating not only the impact of the new system on the children involved, but on their families. It would be reflective, historical in its descriptions of the post-war world and probably, given the high political profile of the selection debate over the years, opinionated.

With these thoughts I approached Paul Davies, who not only liked the idea for Bitesize Books, but immediately, to my delight, said he would be one of the contributors. Finding the other two contributors was not difficult. I am conscious, of course, that there are very high profile examples of the meritocracy in our political system at the moment – Sajid Javid, Dawn Butler and Sadiq Khan to name but three – but these are different, in that as the children of immigrants they were part of the second, later wave of the social adjustment of Britain. I wanted this book to explore what it was like at the beginning of the social mobility experiment, when the Atlee Labour government was in power and things seemed to be looking up for the working class. So I asked two of my acquaintances, one a fellow teacher and the other a poet and television writer, and, I'm pleased to say, they both accepted the challenge.

The contributors were given carte blanche about what and how they wrote about their childhood and school experiences, and there are some unsurprising and some very surprising similarities and differences. In all of them, life for children in the 50s comes alive; it was radio and early television, comics, boy scouts and the freedom to play in the streets without fear, to the back-drop of new council estates being built. But the shadow of the war persists, not only in bomb-sites and rationing and ex-servicemen trying to make a living, but in how it was changing attitudes – dads and grandfathers had fought for a better life for their children and they were determined to get it. The picture is of stable, hard-working families – mums and dads – supportive in their own way of these new opportunities opening up to their children, but at the same time unsure and perplexed about this brave new world which was taking their children, educationally at least, away from them, and very conscious of the cost, financial and emotional.

Primary schools get a good press in all four accounts, but not surprisingly, the 11+ features vividly. It loomed large in our lives as the great divider, the key which unlocked the different life for which our parents (particularly mothers, who were themselves unfulfilled) were ambitious. Grammar school was the million dollar prize; it separated the few from the many and had to be taken seriously, though interestingly, none of us remembers it causing the kind of stress which the modern version apparently causes in those areas where selection still exists. We'd probably have been told to just get on with it and take it in our stride; children don't get stressed!

How we all adapted to the new school is surprisingly different, as is how we see it from this distance. Di and I, both of whom enthusiastically embraced grammar school, with all its idiosyncrasies, describe life there with affection. And ironically, the only so-called 'failure' of the 11+, Barry, writes warmly of his eccentric teachers at his secondary modern, where teaching methods seem to have been more enlightened than those at the grammar schools, which were presumably aping the private schools to which the masters and mistresses must have gone. All three of these contrast dramatically with Paul's account of his seven years of misery, which served only to 'turn success into failure' and caused a sense of betrayal which has never gone away.

With the exception of Paul, the contributors pay homage to a particular teacher who inspired them – a common theme in all literature exploring or exposing the meritocracy. Without those individuals (English teachers in all our cases) there is a feeling that we might not have progressed to university and the professions, that we might not have had the confidence to break out of the traditional expectations of the working class. In all four accounts, however much we might have enjoyed the experience, there is the nagging doubt that we didn't 'really' fit in. In Di's, Barry's and my stories, we have underplayed this, but it forms the main thrust of Paul's narrative, as he describes vividly the 'sheep' and the 'goats', and how he didn't fit into either group.

In the background of all four pieces are the families. It was something I wanted the book to explore, remembering from my PGCE days the work of Marsden and Jackson who concluded in 'Education and the Working Class' (1961) that although grammar schools purportedly existed for clever working class children, in reality those who succeeded were children from very particular kinds of working class families – those influenced either by religion or the trades union movement. And to an extent this theory is borne out in the stories here. The religious aspect was certainly a determining factor in my evangelical family's ambitions, and the political can be seen, if in a lesser way, in Paul's story, whose father worked in the highly unionised London print industry and in Di's, staunch supporters of the Labour Party. There are clearly other factors at play, too, though, one of which seems to be the experience of the war, including the unlikely coincidence of Barry's father and Paul's grandfather having had very similar experiences as prisoners of war.

But whatever their motivation, most of these families were convinced that education meant a 'better life' and they wanted it for their children, whatever the cost. And central to that was the early introduction of books – which play such a huge role in all the stories that they become almost a character in their own right. This is most strikingly described in Barry's opening paragraph, but plays centre stage in them all, even though books were much more scarce then than now, and most of these working class families had little real knowledge of literature.

Regardless of the degree of support from the families, all four stories describe the widening generational gap as we became more educated than our parents – a phenomenon, of course, vividly evoked in the kitchen sink dramas of the 50s, but handled here with more subtlety, sensitivity and affection than in those hard-hitting exposures.

To reply to the question raised by the title of this little book – it can be seen that the four contributors used their educational opportunities well. All four went on to higher education and entered the professions – either into teaching or via teaching to other careers. And for Di, Barry and I, a certain amount of gratitude comes through the pieces – though all politically left of centre and very pro the comprehensive system which followed soon after we left school, we know that the system actually did well by us. It might have been flawed, and left out a whole raft of clever working class children who could have benefitted, but it worked for us and it would be churlish not to appreciate that. We have lived very different lives from those lived by our parents, and we have benefitted financially, socially and culturally. We have bought houses, travelled the world and mixed with a wide range of people from all classes; it must sometimes at least occur to our professional, educated children that they are one generation away from hard manual labour.

Vince Cable, in his excellent introduction to the book, concludes that meritocracy is probably the best, though flawed, way to manage education, because without it we could just be ruled by the elitist, public school gang with no understanding of the rest of society. In this he also recognizes, however, that whatever system of merit we put in place, there will be those who are 'left behind', something in the background of all the pieces, but most powerfully present in Di' story of her sister, and the deep sense of betrayal which pervades Paul's story.

I am very grateful to the three contributors who joined me in reminiscing about their school days and contemplating ideas of meritocracy and social mobility. It was not the intention of the book to add significantly to the great debate about how as a society we organise education, but I am very pleased that, if only in a small way, the informed and strongly held views expressed here might do just that. Perhaps another sub-title to the book could have been 'Why us'? and I think that together, the four pieces go some way to answering the question.

The contributors:

Diana Bruce graduated from the University of Lancaster in 1971 with an English degree and spent the following year in America where she worked as an admin assistant in the University of Colorado admissions office. On return to the UK she took up her deferred PGCE place at the University of London, Goldsmiths' College and began a long and rewarding career teaching in the first purpose-built comprehensive school in Inner London. During two maternity leaves, she juggled part-time teaching, part-time tutoring on the Goldmiths' PGCE English course and part-time working with newly qualified probationary teachers on a local authority Induction programme. In subsequent years, first as Head of English and Media and later as Assistant Head on the Senior Leadership team, her work focused on cross-curricular teaching and learning and coaching staff. In 2009, following retirement from full time work, she was invited to join a National Strategy team at the (then) DCSF working on a project across primary and secondary schools and also joined a consultancy supporting teachers in a range of secondary schools across the south-east. She is currently a governor at a London primary school where she has happily supported pupils and staff in the teaching of English, just for the love of it!

Paul Davies emerged from university in Leeds and Derry with a PhD on the novels of George Eliot and taught in a secondary modern, a grammar school and two large comprehensives, leaving teaching as Senior Teacher and Head of English during the worst years of the Thatcher assault on state education. He joined the IT industry, and spent thirty years in corporate life, latterly as managing director in India. In 2003 he set up his own management consultancy addressing offshoring, outsourcing and globalisation, before becoming a publisher by setting up Bite-Sized Books.

Barry Simner was born near Epsom in Surrey. After failing the Eleven Plus he was educated at the local secondary modern before gaining a place at Surbiton Grammar School. From there he went to The Central School of Speech & Drama and became a teacher in several London schools before ending his career in 1987 as Head of English at The Pimlico School.

His first stage play was performed shortly after at The Salisbury Playhouse and his first TV play, *'Mixing It'*, aired the following year on Channel 4 with Art Malik in the lead. His stage version of the silent movie classic, *'The Cabinet of Doctor Caligari'*, opened at Nottingham playhouse before transferring to a successful run at The Lyric Theatre in Hammersmith.

Barry has written for some of television's most successful drama series including *'The Bill'*, *'Midsomer Murders'* and Britain's first Asian soap, *'Family Pride'*. He was co-creator and principal writer on ITV's hit series *'The Vice'* and his critically acclaimed Irish Drama series, *'Single-Handed'*, won a Best Actor award for Stephen Rea. Barry was twice runner-up in the Arvon/Observer International Poetry Competition. He is an experienced creative writing tutor working for The Arvon Foundation, The Taliesin Trust as well as in universities, schools and colleges. For the last thirty years he has lived in Snowdonia where he was once a mountaineering instructor. He now has trouble climbing the stairs.

After her English degree at Goldsmiths' College, Margaret Peacock decided to teach and stayed on at Goldsmiths' to take a PGCE course. Her first teaching job was at a small London C of E comprehensive in Lambeth, after which she was appointed as Head of English at Kidbrooke, a very large girls' comprehensive in Greenwich. After many happy years there, in 1988 she became Deputy Head at Chestnut Grove School in

Wandsworth, taking up the headship two years' later. Apart from a year's transfer to support a local struggling school, having become an NLE (National Leader in Education), she stayed at Chestnut Grove for 25 years, taking it from a very challenging, underperforming school to a highly successful, popular school which achieved an Ofsted 'Outstanding' in 2008. She is very proud of the fact that many of Chestnut Grove's senior staff are now very successful head teachers in their own right.

Since retirement, she works as a consultant to secondary and primary schools, is a governor of two schools (including one highly selective maths school) and is finding a new career in editing!

Chapter 1

Continuing to Live

Barry Simner

And what's the profit? Only that, in time,
We half-identify the blind impress
All our behavings bear, may trace it home.
But to confess,

On that green evening when our death begins,
Just what it was, is hardly satisfying,
Since it applied only to one man once,
And that one dying.

'Continuing to Live', by Philip Larkin.

We're sitting at my Nan's dining table, Mum, Dad with me between them. I think I'm five years old. Dad's using the bone-handled bread knife to slice open a cardboard box that's just arrived in the post. We don't get many deliveries like this at our house and the box might come in handy so he's being careful not to damage it.

Inside the box is something heavy – eight big books covered in red leather with gold lettering. They've brought a new smell into the house – a smell I will come to love. Slowly dad lifts them out and lays them on the table in front of us. They are the first books we've ever owned – apart from my Rupert Bear annuals and 'Twitchy Whiskers on the Track' which dad reads to me every night before he tucks me up in their double bed –

Nan's in the small room and 'Uncle Jack' (my step grandfather) sleeps in the box room.

I stare at the books, afraid to touch them but then dad looks at me and says, "These are yours – to keep." I don't know exactly what they are but they're obviously precious and very beautiful and Dad's telling me they're mine – "to keep". They are called 'The New Book of Knowledge' and Dad tells me they're really one big book called an encyclopaedia. Sixty-odd years later, they stand on a shelf behind me as I write this – solid red ingots, still unstained and still unblemished cultural icons. I've seen the same set in the homes of other people of my generation so they must have been popular. I think they're the greatest piece of good fortune any child of five could have received as a gift. They are Mum and Dad's investment in me and my future.

No one we know has a television and our only entertainment is the big wireless on the sideboard. So from then on our evenings are spent by the fire, slowly turning the thick pages of The New Book of Knowledge. My favourite pictures are the blue star charts showing the major constellations; the sepia prints of pyramids and one of 'Terra Nova' trapped in the Antarctic ice. Another one I like shows a human mouth like a factory floor, food coming in on a conveyor-belt tongue and workmen with hosepipes and rubber boots hosing down the teeth. We don't make a sound as we look because I think we feel a bit like thieves, too shocked by something they've stolen, to speak.

I like saying the word encyclopaedia. I also like the funny words written on the spines of the books but they're harder to say and I don't know what they mean. They go: 'A-bon, Boo-dew, Dia-grap, Gras-lom, Lon-pap, Par-sop, Sou-zwi, and Index'. sometimes I chant them to myself before I go to sleep – an incantation, a charm against the dark. "A-bon, Boo-dew", I mumble as I doze off with my feet against the stone hot-water bottle. Nan tells me that Mum and Dad are paying half-a-crown a week for the books on something called 'never- never'. Two shillings and sixpence from their small wages to give me possession of these syllables of power.

When my own daughter was five, we bought her a new 'Britannica' as our 'investment' in her future. The day it arrived a man came to clean the carpets and spotting Britannica proudly displayed on the shelves said, "Yow can get all that on a computer for a few quid now." He was right of course. Within a year the whole thing went on-line and access to an entire universe of knowledge became available to anyone with 'a few quid' to spare. But that was still many years in the future and throughout my childhood 'The New Book of Knowledge' remained the fount of all wisdom in our house. "Look it up", dad would say whenever I asked him a tricky question. "Look in your books". It's what I still do instinctively.

Shortly after the books arrived, Mum took me to join our new local library. She and Dad were already members and once a week I went with her for the ritual of returning the books they'd read, getting the tickets stamped and carrying off a new clutch. It was a trip Mum always dressed for and carried her best handbag – the one that smelt of Coty Powder, lipstick and cigarettes. I walked next to her wearing my new school cap from Buckland Road Infants.

Library books were arriving in the house regularly by now. It didn't seem odd to me though I noticed that my cousin, David, who lived along the road, and my other friend Roger, didn't seem to have any books in their houses at all, only a daily paper or a copy of Woman's Weekly. Our library books were treated with the same reverence as the encyclopaedia. You didn't fold the pages or risk spilling food on them or touch them with dirty hands or, god forbid, write in them. They were as much ornamental as functional, beautiful as well as practical. I wonder if that's how some travelling salesman, probably an ex-serviceman like dad, had persuaded him to sign up for the offer.

Or perhaps he'd spotted a bright little boy hiding in the passageway and told Dad how much he'd benefit from the small expense.

In 1947, when I was born, Dad had been home from Germany for two years returning to the same bench, in the same engineering factory he'd started in at fourteen.

He'd joined the Kings' Royal Rifle Corps in 1939 and was immediately posted to France to try to halt the German advance on Dunkirk. The Rifle Brigades immediately found themselves cut off in Calais with no chance of escape. They fought for four days, losses were heavy and they eventually found themselves with their backs to the sea with no hope of rescue. Churchill's orders conveyed to their Commanding Officer in a famous telegram were that there was to be no surrender; they were to continue fighting until the last man fell. Exposed to constant attack from Stuka dive bombers and the XX Panzer Division, cut off by the sea, they eventually collapsed without having surrendered on Sunday 26th April 1940.

Dad spent the next five years as a prisoner of war in various camps in Poland building railways until the Germans, without warning, began rounding up all their prisoners and marching them back towards Germany to escape the advancing Allied and Russian forces. This was during the winter of 1945-46, one of the coldest of the Twentieth Century with temperatures falling to minus twenty and sometimes forty degrees below zero. Dad walked a thousand miles from Gdansk on the Baltic coast into Germany before the German surrender when the RAF flew him home in an old 'Dakota'. Photographs taken when I was born two years later show him still clearly underweight and suffering from the stomach ulcers that plagued him for the rest of his life. Thousands of men had frozen to death or been shot by the roadside on those 'death marches' but somehow he'd managed to survive. His best friend throughout his imprisonment was Ted McCready from Sidney Street in

Whitechapel and whenever Ted came to visit he'd give me a shilling and tell me, without explaining how, that dad had saved his life. *"Every man thinks meanly of himself for never having been a soldier".*

Reminders of the war were everywhere in the early fifties – not in the bomb-damaged buildings which were mostly miles away in central London, but in the blind, legless or disfigured ex-servicemen who seemed to be everywhere. Men in sinister-looking wheelchairs worked by a sort of upside-down bicycle were a common sight; men selling brushes door-to-door; men on clumsy wooden crutches; men with scars or limbs missing. My dad, one of the 'lucky ones', still wore his battledress for digging the garden and kept his trousers up with the black leather belt he'd bartered from a German guard. He'd made the buckle himself from a piece of brass and a bent nail and I still have it. Most people's dads had 'done their bit' for their country but dad, like many others, hardly spoke of it – except to make us laugh. His favourite tales involved getting one over on the humourless Germans in some way. Once, the entire camp of several thousand men were forced to watch a fire drill by the camp fire brigade in front of a visiting General. When the alarm was raised by ringing a loud bell, all the smallest men available ran from their huts wearing cardboard helmets and carrying tiny hoses and very small ladders which didn't reach the windows. The entire camp was helpless with laughter and punished. The point was to humiliate the enemy.

Mum and Dad were married as soon as soon as he returned. He was twenty-four and she was twenty-three and I still have every devoted letter he wrote to her while he was away. By the time I was born, they were living with my Nan near Epsom having been bombed out of their home in Peckham.

This was a nice little thirties 'semi' near Nan's sister. Many of the neighbours were already settled, owner-occupiers and better off in many respects, perhaps with a motorbike or even a car parked in the yard. Our neighbour, 'Biff' Cook, kept chickens which pecked my fingers when I tried to feed them. Jack found refuge in the wonderfully named local pub, 'The Bones Gate' which had another memorable poem inscribed on its gate.

This gate hangs well,
And hinders none.
Refresh and pay
And travel on.

Jack took full advantage of the invitation.

Nan's house had a back garden which led into miles of woods and farmland where we could go blackberrying and scrumping. I learnt the names of trees and birds and was free to wander with my cousin, David, wherever we liked, always with a penknife and stick in hand. Step out of our front door and you'd be in the new suburbs with buses and a half-hourly train service into London – that was the way I didn't like going. Out of our back door and in twenty yards you'd be lost in luminous woodland dense with bluebells and fields that stretched for miles into the Surrey countryside. The train journey into London was a voyage into our smoky and huddled family past; the walk into the woods was an expedition into a mysterious future and was where I began to feel most at home.

The nineteen fifties were an interlude of quiet before the woods and fields, already being eyed up by canny speculators, were swallowed by 'Greater London'. The farms and barns were converted into desirable housing. The medieval 'Stew Ponds', where you could skate and risk falling through the ice in winter, became a country park with warning signs everywhere. The 'Bricky', that unfathomable and weed-choked pool where we fished for newts and frogs, became polluted and filled with rubbish. The zoo where we could sneak in for free across the fields, became something called 'The World of Adventures'. We were lucky to live there before it became an anti-Eden of estates, factories and service roads with no links to its rural past.

One unique feature of the area remained to dominate our lives and fill our imaginations. Since the beginning of the Twentieth Century, London had exiled its insane to what Ian Sinclair memorably calls, "an archipelago of lunatic asylums", five between Epsom and my home two miles away and their names still haunt me: The Manor, Horton, St Ebba's, West Park, and the ominously named Long Grove. We became used to seeing the patients (many of them ex-servicemen suffering from what was to become PTSD) wandering through the woods and fields and our rambles were peopled with odd characters, troubling behaviours and the mutterings of the insane. One patient had created an elaborate 'shrine' around an oak tree and decorated it with string, bottle tops, brightly coloured rags and sweet wrappers. On one of our teenage adventures we found a crazy old woman standing in a ditch, half naked, covered in mud and weeds like some elderly Ophelia. We grew up in a Midsummer Night's Dreamscape, surreal, frightening and beautiful where anything was possible and anything might suddenly materialise: lost gazers into vacancy; speechless petitioners with out-stretched hands; sad refugees unable to make themselves understood; rough sleepers in orchards or old pillboxes. Any landscapes can appear magical to a child's eye but there can have been few places where the ordinary coexisted with the strange as in that pastoral suburban paradise.

For adults newly-arrived from London, it must have seemed a dark and threatening place lying uncomfortably close to our bedroom window. Stories of peculiar events and sightings were commonplace and only whispered among my aunts and neighbours. One night we huddled in the kitchen with the lights off while doctors in white coats ran along our back alley chasing an escaped maniac. At least, that's what Nan said she saw and I believed her. All the same, we carried on with our blackberry picking, scrumping and exploring regardless and no one was ever murdered or disappeared.

My first school, Buckland Road Infants, was ten minutes' walk away and Moor Lane Junior Mixed only fifteen. And every one of those walks to and from school (four times a day because I went home for dinner) was an adventure. It's common to think of fifties' Britain as a place of dreary conformity, especially for children. In fact many of us had far more space and liberty than today. We were free of constant adult surveillance, largely unsupervised and could wander, disappear and 'get up' to things. In short, we could be mischievous and 'adventures' became what we plotted for and planned our days around.

It was a small, cosy school for children from the new estates which were being built all round London and the big cities. Our parents were young and many mums, like mine, still worked in the local factories where they'd been employed doing war work.

I was part of a small group taken by Mrs Thompson for special reading classes in the staff room where it was warm and smelt of coffee; but whether I was there because I was especially good at reading or needed extra help, I never discovered. Certainly I was usually the first child chosen to read out loud in class but that might have been my obvious eagerness to show off.

At Moor Lane, I remember none of today's obsessive testing or constant assessment and it wasn't until I was eleven that I even heard the word 'exam'. Apparently, we were going to sit something called 'The Eleven Plus' the next day. Given that we soon discovered it might change our lives forever, it seems odd that we'd had no preparation and no coaching. I certainly don't remember my parents discussing it. So it was one morning in the summer term, that we sat at our usual desks in our usual classroom and tried to answer some questions on arithmetic, writing and general knowledge. I don't remember how long it took but I do remember I couldn't wait to get outside and run about because the sun was shining and I wanted to show off to Linda Hook – or possibly Susan Parker. Linda had blonde hair and I liked her best but on other days I liked Susan. That was The Eleven Plus over and done with.

The reckoning came some weeks later when the Headmistress, Miss Charlcraft (severe grey hair, specs) called the whole school into the hall and read the results. The children who'd passed, she said, would be going to the grammar school while the rest of us were going to somewhere called a Secondary Modern School. When we were fourteen, some of us might go to something called 'a technical school' where they could learn engineering, draughtsmanship or typing. I never heard mention of Technical Schools again and never knew anyone who attended one.

After reading out the results, Miss Charlcraft dismissed us in rows and we filed out of the hall. But she'd obviously made a mistake. Bob Tomkins had passed but I'd failed. How had that happened? And what about Robert Webster? Why was he going to the grammar school while I was being sent to the Secondary a couple of miles down the road? And my best friend, Graham… he was far cleverer than me but he'd failed as well. What had gone wrong? Days before, we'd all been the same. We lived and played on the same streets, we had similar families and came from similar homes. We were the same ordinary post-war children. Some of us were better at reading or arithmetic or could run faster or were better at football but we were the same children from good homes. Something remarkable had obviously happened to us without our being aware of it – something called 'selection' at Eleven Plus.

A couple of weeks later, I was told I'd been granted a reprieve. Either I'd been what they called a 'borderline' fail or, far more likely, the authorities were short of their grammar school quota for September 1959 because Miss Charlcraft called me into her office and told me I'd been given a second chance to sit the exam. I sat the exam again – and failed again. Obviously I wasn't clever enough.

Years later in my first student flat, I started my own 'library' with shelves made from rough planks balanced on bricks and it was about then that the dreams began. I'm standing in a Grand house, a mansion or a castle but it's abandoned and ruinous. There are threadbare tapestries hanging from the walls, peeling plaster, holes in the ceilings. I climb a high, crumbling staircase, open a door and discover a vast library. The shelves are stocked with books but they're all in danger from the rain blowing in through broken windows and cracked slates. Many are already lying on the floor, sodden and ruined and only I can save them so I begin lifting the oldest and most fragile but as soon as I touch them they fall apart in my arms. Now it's getting dark. How many can I carry away before I can't see? Three? Two? None? Fifty years later and I'm still having the dream.

Meanwhile, the dream library was getting bigger and fuller and still I could only carry away one or two volumes at a time. Perhaps there was another lesson to be taken from the New Book of Knowledge – one that was harder to accept. The voice I heard whenever I woke from yet another dream and another botched attempt to rescue the precious books, was perhaps reminding me that I'd failed again. "You don't know enough," it said. "In fact, you don't really 'know' anything". The authentic mark of the autodidact: fear of public exposure as a phoney. Is this the 'wound' I had to carry? The scar my early failure at Eleven Plus left on me? What Philip Larkin calls, *"The blind impress all our behavings bear"*?

The late Christopher Hitchens explained the often yawning gap between his public pronouncements and his private behaviour as being the result of 'keeping two sets of accounts': one for himself and the other for 'the taxman'. Failure at eleven plus went straight into my 'taxable' accounts and became the start of my story of finding that the world is an unfair place where I could find injustice everywhere. Resentment at the unfairness of the system could make me a latter-day 'Jude the Obscure', the victim of a biased system, unfairly denied my rightful place at a grammar school. Wasn't I a 'victim' of selection, living proof of its pernicious and lasting effects? It was a powerful story and served me well in a career as a fire-breathing radical activist. Faced with any argument in favour of selective schooling, I could produce my trump card and describe my own long struggle against 'the system' before the final recognition of my genius. Ignoring the fact that this was all fabricated, I could file it in my private tax account while still holding onto my credentials as a genuine 'working class hero'.

Fleetwood County Secondary Boys' School was my school. Light and airy with big windows and spacious gardens; a big playing field, a hall with a big stage, a gym, bicycle sheds, a railway station next door and a bus stop outside. Arranged around three sides of a central playground, were an assembly hall, workshops, technical labs and airy classrooms. An efficient and orderly school. What stopped it from also being a dull and uninspiring place were the teaching staff. Some of the older staff had taught before the war but a lot had joined the profession after an Emergency Recruitment Campaign aimed specifically at ex-servicemen and women. These were often experienced people, often with a military background and had been marked by it in some way, either physically or emotionally. Some had become comically militarised but service life had also given them a far broader experience of the world and its possibilities than civvy-street ever could. The best of them had joined the profession because they wanted to inspire and prepare a new generation for the better world they'd fought for. They had real experience of how people performed under stress, knew about human frailty and how to inspire, encourage and lead. Perhaps crucially, they understood what it felt like to be frightened, uncertain and try to learn new skills under pressure.

Their eccentricities brought out our childish cruelty. Mr Mason (Physics) had clearly developed some form of Tourette's Syndrome which made him burst out with strange sounds or inappropriate mutterings – especially if we were working quietly. Dr Turner (RE) a fundamentalist Christian, could be provoked into an uncontrollable rage by any mention of Darwin and the theory of evolution, particularly that flying reptile, archaeopteryx.

It was an all-male environment and the eccentricities of the staff were legendary, certainly tolerated and perhaps even encouraged by the head for their unpredictability and ability to entertain big classes of unruly boys. Mr Sanders had served with the RAF in India, drove vintage cars and smoked enthusiastically – like his exotic cars. He taught English, inspired my love of literature and poetry and ran a flourishing drama club that staged variety productions every Christmas. His most ambitious was a full-scale production of Delibe's ballet, Coppelia in which I 'danced' the part of Franz – and this in an all-boys' school.

Mr Butcher (History) made a cross-bow and demonstrated it by firing across our heads a bolt which buried itself in the wall. He also taught us how to make black powder from puff balls and used it to fire a musket on the football pitch. One of Mr Mason's Science classes involved the construction of a working coal-fired gas plant which took up the entire front bench of the lab but exploded suddenly showering us with coal dust and tar. When Philip Crick (Maths and a published poet) sat himself next to me during a lesson where I was bored and struggling to understand, I expected another futile lecture on logarithms. Instead, he suggested I'd be better off writing my poems than doing maths. I took him at his word and a few years later, found myself reading alongside Philip at a poetry event in a club near Oxford Street. My first professional gig.

Unlike so many children today, I don't remember feeling anxious or 'stressed' by school. I wasn't much interested in sports but I enjoyed cross-country running, joined the drama club and The Boy Scouts where I was a Patrol Leader and enthusiastic collector of badges, especially for anything outdoors, or adventurous. It would be hard to over-estimate the influence of organisations like The Scouts in the lives of boys in particular: weekly meetings; weekend camps; 'Bob-a-job' weeks; fetes and fundraisers to buy kit. Our lives outside of school were shaped by the organisation which I still think encouraged a sense of responsibility and purpose – probably deeply unfashionable now. We were all unquestioning loyalists because that's what our parents were, proud of our country and, when I became Head Boy of the school I was proud of my badge.

How different was I really from other boys? I think quite a lot. I existed on the periphery of lots of groups working my dual accounting system. Hanging around the Youth Club at night but going home to write poetry or record radio plays on Saturday mornings with my best friend Graham. Being a 'Mod' on Fridays, a Bohemian on Mondays. Practising various roles but never committing to one group. 'Oddities' and if it weren't for a few inspiring teachers who gave me the ambition to hope for something different I would certainly have drifted into a job as a clerical assistant in the Ordnance Survey down the road.

The truth is that failure at Eleven Plus didn't necessarily condemn one to a life of failure. Other boys had a range of interests and abilities and many couldn't wait to get out of the school environment which I clearly enjoyed. I liked learning things and I was generally polite and biddable, if cheeky. Only in my last sixth-form school photo do I appear scowling fashionably beneath a Beatle fringe. So I can't claim that failure was a sort of intellectual circumcision. On the contrary, I think it did me a lot of good. That old tri-partite system, far from being rigid and unyielding was very flexible and if, like me, you managed to scrape through some O Levels you could even move to the Sixth Form of the local grammar school. This was largely thanks to John Sanders, who coached me so that I passed just enough papers to qualify me for a transfer to the Grammar School and became one of two boys to be offered an interview.

I met Mr Forward, Deputy Head of Surbiton Grammar School, on the steps of the grand but shabby stucco Victorian mansion that served as the main building, one warm September afternoon. He was tall, wearing an old academic gown liberally dusted with chalk and had white hair. Looking through my pathetic clutch of results, he saw I'd passed something called Greek Lit in Translation (considered an easy additional subject). He asked how well I knew 'The Iliad'. I had a good memory for poetry and could recite the first lines in English: "Sing Goddess, the wrath of Achilles, Peleus' son…". He replied with what I think were the same lines in Greek: 'Μῆνιν ἄειδε θεὰ Πηληϊάδεω Ἀχιλῆος'. A man who knew Greek! As we spoke of Agamemnon, Menelaus and Aeschylus, I felt almost intoxicated. I was sitting in the sunshine discussing the founding texts of Western civilization with a man who might have been Socrates himself.

I was flattered that he seemed interested in what I was saying. "Ignore the love story. Why do you think they really went to war?" I stumbled through some half-baked ideas about trade routes and strategic cities in the Mediterranean and tried out the theory (which I'd read somewhere) that the conflict arose because Troy stood at the crossroads of important trade routes. I mentioned H.D.F. Kitto's Pelican Classic, 'The Greeks' and Mary Renault's popular novel, 'The Mask of Apollo'. He seemed most intrigued by the Renault and, after a pause, told me he would write to my parents that day offering me a place in Villiers House, Lower Sixth Arts where I'd be studying English, History and Music. (I had no idea at the time, but the school 'houses' were all named after banks – a clear indication of the sort of careers we were expected to follow.)

The bell rang for lesson change and I watched Mr Forward disappear under the cypress trees before I ran down the hill to catch the bus home. There was a school outfitters near the station where I stopped to buy a tie and a new school badge. At home, I tore off my blazer and handed it to Mum who took the news with her usual phlegmatic, "That's nice", picked off the badge of my Secondary School and sewed on the gold Lion of St Mark, the badge of The County Grammar School.

In fact Surbiton Grammar would have been considered a third-rate Grammar School with poor facilities and within a few years it was forced to join a couple of secondary-mods and become 'comprehensive'. But at the time I didn't see its failings.

The work of turning me from one of the 'estate' kids into an intellectual snob was begun, not by the grammar school, but much earlier in my secondary school. Somehow I'd got hold of the idea that I belonged somewhere else, somewhere more prestigious or simply 'posher'. I began to hate the way mum and my aunts laughed at Kathleen Ferrier singing 'Blow the Wind Southerly' on the wireless and called her singing 'painful'. As a family we certainly couldn't be described as posh despite the fact that my school report made a point of mentioning that, "Barry speaks very well". Where did that come from? Always an enthusiastic mimic, I was probably imitating people I'd heard on the wireless but I remember that I couldn't wait to get out of what I increasingly thought of as the wrong 'speech community'. Not just a place where people spoke with a different accent but spoke about more interesting things.

It was a feeling (common enough amongst kids becoming more educated than their parents) that grew throughout my teenage years. Was I ashamed of Mum and Dad? Never ashamed, but perhaps too easily embarrassed by their obvious awkwardness in some situations. They were kind and 'agreeable' people who wanted to be liked but didn't want to be thought to be getting above themselves. Modest would, I suppose, describe them best. No one in the family had ever achieved anything remarkable, been to university, won a medal or done anything unusual but then neither had anyone been divorced, arrested or appeared in the Sunday papers – until I blotted the family record by appearing at Bow Street Magistrates Court after a demo in Grosvenor Square.

We weren't religious, even now I've no idea how my parents voted and I don't remember them expressing any strong political opinions. I do remember my dad finding I'd bought a copy of 'Old Moore's Almanack' and throwing it on the fire because it was "superstitious nonsense". Apart from our library books, the everyday reading matter in our house was similar to everyone else's: 'The Evening News', 'The Sunday People' and 'Woman's Own'. Our regular listening on the wireless, 'Music While You Work', 'The Goon Show' and 'Round the Horne' before Sunday lunch. As an enthusiastic Boy Scout I was proud to carry the flag to church once a month and march behind the band. But one day I seem to have been in short trousers and a khaki uniform and the next I'm wearing a Beatle Jacket at the Youth Club dance but still leading a secret 'inner life'. Either things were changing very fast or I was already " keeping those two sets of accounts". Or, more likely, it was because the whole of society was starting to do the same.

What's difficult to convey is the growing sense of living on the cusp of something big. It was 'the Age of Aquarius', after all, and there was a palpable sense that my parents' generation were slowly fading while ours was in the ascendant. Nothing unusual in that, but there really was a growing excitement and energy abroad; something our parents' generation had been denied by the war. After years of hardship, deprivation and abstinences of all kinds, what must they have made of us? My dad seems to have had only one woman in his life, my mother, while I thought myself unlucky if there was only one a week. Why didn't he hate his promiscuous little shit of a son for it? He was a kind and generous man who knew that with a different education he would have had a very different life and that's what he wanted for me. Bitterness and resentment were completely foreign emotions to him.

For a couple of years in the late sixties we were both students. After sixth form and a year waiting for an audition, I was finally at drama school in London where my old English teacher, John Sanders, had suggested I apply. Dad, meanwhile, had been sent by his firm on a three-year 'sandwich- course' at the local polytechnic to study 'management'. While I was poncing around in a pair of tights, he was buying himself a leather briefcase, a dozen coloured pens and a slide-rule while Mum bought him a copy of 'Fowler's Modern English Usage'. It wasn't an easy change of status for him. He would still be working at Samuel Jones and Co. in Camberwell where he'd been at school with many of the staff so there was understandable envy of his good fortune.

Within a few years they'd made the transition from working to middle class and in another few years he became a director and finally Managing Director of the company he'd worked for all his life. I enjoyed watching them adapting, sometimes awkwardly, to their new roles. Now they were going to functions, dinner-dances, and enjoying a modestly prosperous life. Dad even bought himself a set of golf clubs but found that all-important social side a step too far. But he was clever and they were both hard-working and deserved the promotion and the respect it brought. I remember visiting him at the works and saw how proud he was looking down at his new Jaguar parked inside the gates that he'd walked through as a boy of fourteen.

And I was proud of him though my grudging and ungenerous politics probably didn't let me show it as much as I should have. We were one of the most fortunate generations in history but also one of the most ungrateful.

Ask most people what they most remember from school and they mention, not an exam result, but an inspiring teacher. It is something universally attested to and yet, as a nation, we're still addicted to grading children by means of a medieval system. Ask employers what they look for in a recruit and they list articulacy, presentation, creativity, imagination and social skills – qualities that appear nowhere in the curriculum. Trying to score them is absurd.

Arguments about the proper way to educate children have dominated my early career as a teacher and my later career as a writer. There's no sign of this obsession ending any time soon. And this is because we've never been able to make up our minds about what schools are for or what we want them to do. Whichever side of the argument we come down on, we remain obsessed with exams and grading because they're easy things to score and compare nationally and across countries. Without any clear idea of what a good education is, governments, Gradgrind-like, seize on 'facts', and the more facts they can harvest, the better. They think data will provide the evidence they require to control the entire system of incentives, rewards and penalties. It's an absurd belief because most of what children learn in school is un-measurable.

I've heard it argued that the real iniquity of the Eleven-Plus was that it was far too crude a measure of a child's ability. That if it had been more scientific it might have been fairer. On the other hand, it's said that it was fundamentally wicked to select children on the basis of a rudimentary I.Q. test. Did it really condemn me and thousands of children like me to think of ourselves as failures, second rate, unworthy of a 'proper' education? Were there many "mute inglorious Miltons" permanently overlooked? Or did the system quite reasonably favour clever children from poorer homes, giving them the opportunity to thrive by offering the chance of a university place and a professional career?

Of course, selection did both – favoured some and damaged others. Some must have withered to allow others to flourish. But in order to flourish, the child needs to be ready and receptive and that's something that's impossible to arrange. Why me and not my cousin David? David lived next door, was the same age and at the same school with the same teachers but he was condemned to edging lawns and weeding the flowerbeds while I sat inside in the warm conjugating French verbs? But then David, was by nature shy, while my mum, younger by a few years, eagerly embraced her suburban new life.

Why do some kids 'get' what the teacher's saying while others from similar backgrounds, never do? Finally one ends up looking at the only real evidence we have – our own individual experience. If we're fortunate, we might find a teacher who can inspire and show us a path. I was lucky to have a number of them. People like my history teacher, Mr Butcher. One day he brought a piece of red tile into class – something he'd found lying in a field near the school. Passing it round the room, he said, "This is a Roman tile." Then he took a small silver coin from his pocket and announced, "This is a Roman coin." After passing the coin round, he held it up and dropped it theatrically onto the tile. "Did you hear that sound? That was a Roman sound." Probably a trick he'd performed a hundred times before. A bit of well-rehearsed teacherly magic? Of course. But an absolutely unforgettable moment that dissolved a thousand years of history and shone a bright light onto a distant past. At least it did for me – and perhaps only me. And that's the point.

Larkin is surely right when he says in the final stanza of 'Learning to Live', after long searching for the key to our own success or failure in life – "the blind impress all our behavings bear," the knowledge will be unlikely to satisfy us, since it applies, "only to one man once, and that man dying".

Chapter 2

It's Still Home and They Are Home Truths

Diana Milnes

My name was Diana Margaret Milnes; born on September 12th 1949 in Worksop, Nottinghamshire, where I lived until I was 18. The surname has changed – twice – and I've moved away from there in many ways, but the older I get the more those years of childhood and schooling tell me about myself now. It's still home and they are home truths.

I was eight and my sister Trudy was 5 when we moved into a newly built council house on a post-war estate still being developed on the fringes of town – what Alan Garner later, shockingly, described in *The Weirdstone of Brasingamen* as 'a rash of houses...like a ring of pink scum.'

Our home was on Chesterton Drive and the whole estate's names paid tribute to the English literary canon. Cowper Close. Milton Drive. Shakespeare Street. Behind our road there were fields and beyond our immediate area there were unfinished streets leading into flattened brown land yet to be developed, but for my mum and dad it was the rainbow's pot of gold and, for a while, my sister and I had the joy of cows at the bottom of our garden . Before that we had lived in a small 3 up 2 down cottage by the Chesterfield canal which ran through town.

17, Bridge Terrace. Condemned before the war, it had been re-let because of the housing shortage. No gas, no hot running water, no bathroom and no garden. Outside: a washhouse, a lavatory and a communal yard; inside, rising damp. My dad had made it as comfortable as possible and introduced beauty by transforming one whole wall of their bedroom into a hand-painted mural of a rural scene. A cottage in a woodland setting with flowers in the garden. And my sister and I thought bathing in a tin bath in front of the fire was cosy. Also, our mother's parents lived just across the yard and a well to do family owned a business making ice cream not much further away in the other direction so we had a whole world of family and friends-with-connections on our doorstep. We kids didn't have to worry about how to keep the house warm and free of mice but I know now my mother was desperate.

Eventually, my sister's chronic bronchitis and a GP who fought our corner saw my parents secure the move to the Kilton housing estate in 1957. A brand new three-bedroomed house with gardens front and back - dry, bright, airy, with running hot water and, for my mother, that most blessed of all things - a bathroom. To this day, and she's now 99, she remembers the powerful feelings of relief and gratitude that swept over her when they put the key in the lock. She lived there for 61 years and only moved out in 2018 when vascular dementia moved in.

My father, Howard, came from a Whitwell family, across the county border in Derbyshire. Organist and Choirmaster in the Wesleyan Chapel, my Grandad Milnes was a man who'd had his name in the paper for musical achievements but never made a great living from his considerable craftsmanship in sign-writing and decorating. His small business failed when he hadn't the stamina for collecting money owed from customers unwilling, or unable, to pay. My dad inherited the creative skills. His double bass lived in our dining room and did good service at weekends when he played in the local Palais dance band to earn extra money for our holidays. He wore evening dress on those nights like a uniform and it wasn't until years later that I learned it was the badge of the well–to–do at prestigious events. He was a very fine, meticulous painter and decorator but – also like his father - no businessman and so always worked for others and paid the price in low wages and unrewarded talent. His last years were spent painting equally meticulous copies of scenic photographs in oils on anything he could convert into a canvas; his work shed - our outhouse - a shrine to well-organised and industrious craftsmanship.

My mother, Joyce, had left school at 14. Her wages were needed at home. My grandma was a well-read and sharp-minded Yorkshire woman who always took pride in her general knowledge and, after going blind, listened to audio books until the day she died at 96, but mum was expected to work. She did her three years' apprenticeship as a hairdresser and after her war years as a sergeant in ATS signals carried on until retirement. She picked up the pieces of her broken education at the age of 60 when she went to the local tech and began a 15 year gallop through several O levels, A levels, the foundation year of an Open University degree and a blissful summer school at Durham. The impact that educational directions and missed chances had made on the lives of her extended family wasn't lost on her and the last big piece of work she did was for the local history group: a survey of educational developments in Bassetlaw from the turn of the 20th century. We had it typed and bound.

When we lived at Bridge Terrace and continuing after we moved to Chesterton Drive, my sister and I attended a local C of E primary school in town. My father was a lifelong atheist and didn't approve of the Christian ethos but mother's will prevailed and we went. I thrived, Trudy didn't. A dreadful bout of scarlet fever at five years old, just after she started there, took her into an isolation hospital and a long period of recuperation. When she came back to school she was lost. I was three years ahead of her, loving it all, and she was speedily and unfairly judged to be 'not like Diana'. Behind the others in her class, she received no extra help and was instead encouraged to play in the Wendy house.

With no advance warning from the school, my parents were shocked to receive a letter from Notts County Council requesting them to bring my sister to an education centre in Worksop for assessment tests to decide if she could continue her education in a mainstream school.

The fury that evoked in my mother is something I'll never forget. She marched into school with a book in her hand and challenged the Headmistress to listen to her child read aloud – Trudy had been reading at home fluently – and her response: 'The little monkey," spoke volumes about her views on both academic ability and child psychology. My parents' bitter complaint to Notts County Council did result in a letter of reprimand being sent to St Anne's for not having alerted them first, but this was little compensation and changed nothing in terms of the school's attitude to supporting a child in need.

My sister stayed on at the school and, in retrospect, we both see now that a move to the newly built primary school on Kilton would have been so much better for her, but our parents wanted to keep us together. They couldn't have foreseen how that one awful episode would set her on a course which affected her life chances and put a barrier of academic achievement between us that we couldn't surmount.

I was ten during the final year at St Anne's, but officially too young to transfer when it came to moving on to secondary school. At that time, if a child hadn't turned 11 by August 24th they could not begin the secondary phase so, as a September–born child, I had to repeat the last year - a dubious privilege. I saw my peer group disappear to pastures new and had to adjust to welcoming a batch of other, younger children into 'my' class. Learning came easy, and it was literally learning by rote a lot of the time so I was well ahead. A good memory was key. I enjoyed all the 11+ prep work we did and the daily recitations of the times tables, which was just as well when I had to do so much of it in this repeat year. Teachers were not burdened by the challenges of differentiation in the 1950s. I was also one of a select few allowed to make tea for the teachers and lead the banging of board rubbers on the back fence on Friday afternoons. Slates and chalk: yesterday's A4 white boards and marker pens.

Meanwhile, Trudy was forever seen by teachers as Diana's less able sister and underachieved accordingly. My parents, desperate not to have her compare herself to me, downplayed her academic struggles and reassured her it was perfectly fine to be 'different'. I saw the self-fulfilling prophecy I later learned about on the PGCE course played out before my eyes.

Talking together about this now, as we frequently do, we both see clearly when and how those different directions were set in place and I marvel at my sister's lack of bitterness. We also remember the school's bizarre dinnertime arrangements which had additional serious consequences for her.

Every day, in order to cross the boys' playground to get to the separate building which housed the dining hall, we girls had to climb through a gap in a wooden creosoted fence separating our playground from theirs. I can see it now. The gap was rough-edged and narrow and although a teacher supervised the queue it didn't stop the pushing. One day my sister, at the front of the queue and small, fell beneath a pile of other children. She remembers a teacher, Mrs Wood, carrying her to our grandparents' house. The doctor was sent for and he took her immediately to hospital in his own car. She had concussion. No health and safety in the 1950s - or compensation. She had more time away from school to recover and fell further behind.

There were, however, some very happy times for me at St Anne's. I was a show-off and a mimic. At playtime, on a small raised platform located at one end of the girls' playground, a friend and I would entertain anyone who'd listen with performances as Hilda Baker (me) and her stooge (my friend). This was a well-known television double act at the time and –

like all comics - Hilda had stock phrases which she would churn out to the delight of her audiences. One was 'She knows, you know!' My audiences were no less appreciative and I would float back to the classroom buoyed up by the applause of other 7 year olds.

And the Christmas plays were always longed-for opportunities for me to perform, competing often for the leading role which required a good memory for line-learning. My grandma would pedal away on her Singer treadle machine to run up whatever costume was needed and, one year, invented out of wire and tinsel the fairy tiaras the girls all wore. She made Trudy a pretty outfit the one year she was given a line to speak and, strangely, she still has the dwarf costume she wore, reluctantly, another year.

Grandma's piece de resistance was the costume I was going to wear as Coppelia the Christmas my sister was diagnosed with scarlet fever. I can still see my father walking into the hall during the dress rehearsal, having a quiet word with the teacher in charge and taking me off the stage to begin 3 weeks' quarantine. Self-centred as usual, all I could think of was the lost chance to be a star and as my sister was wheeled down our front path on a stretcher the fact she was clutching my own teddy bear – later incinerated – added to the misery.

Some of our teachers had particular enthusiasms. Mrs Bradbury had us all dancing with Bacca pipes and performing at local events; Mrs Wood trained us to choral-speak for Music and Drama competitions. I had to do solo numbers, learning how to recite chunks of prose to adjudicators. One Just So story extract began, 'And then the Ethiopian...' I had no idea who an Ethiopian might be but I chirruped away and did quite well.

I haunted Worksop library at weekends. We had books at home, many dating back decades, and my dad's special shelf of mighty tomes... the big dictionary, the health encyclopaedia, the Readers Digest condensed novels. But at Worksop library I found all of Enid Blyton and off I went. And comics. Bunty on Tuesdays and Eagle on Fridays (for my dad actually). And plenty of my own story writing. English was always going to be my subject and when I passed the 11+ and told the Head Mistress of my new school at interview how much I loved Enid Blyton I was shocked when she said, "We'll soon sort that out."

I was one of a small group of Worksop girls who travelled the eight miles a day to the High School for Girls in Retford; the last group to be allowed to go there before Worksop was taken out of its catchment area. By 1961 big new secondary schools were being built on the outskirts of Worksop. A County Secondary Technical School had opened in 1956; a grammar school joined it on the same campus in 1963 and alongside both was the Cavendish, a secondary modern school which my sister would later attend. These were the forerunners of amalgamated comprehensives in the 1970s and they would be accommodating all Worksop's eleven year old pupils.

At Retford we were like incomers. All the other girls came from the town itself or the outlying villages. Many of them had attended prep schools and the majority didn't come from backgrounds like mine. In comparison to Worksop, which was then primarily a mining town, Retford was gentrified. The High School centred around an imposing Victorian main building with modern appendages and a couple of large residential houses converted into a science lab and accommodation for the sixth form. I loved the smell of it. Polished floors and staircases. The school grounds bordered on to the same canal which ran through Worksop but at this point it had become leafy, pretty, and the Art Room overlooked it, with steps leading down. Tennis courts and a gymnasium. I thought I'd landed at Malory Towers.

There were 2 forms of entry and I was in the upper band, on my own with no one from St Anne's in my class. We were seated alphabetically for all lessons and the girl I was placed beside had had a tragic experience in the summer, losing both her parents in a car accident. I had no idea how to manage this and she was understandably distant when I tried to make friends. The two girls in front were also strange to me. One had been living in Malaya – a country I'd never heard of - and the other was just gently different from any of the girls I'd grown up with at St Anne's. I knew instinctively that they weren't on any wave-length I'd recognise. Neither would have heard of Hilda Baker. I was lonely and all the confidence built up through the primary years ebbed away.

And first-formers were taught their place very rapidly through the dining room experience. Younger pupils had to take turns to be 'floaters'. This meant lining up during first sitting and being assigned to fill in gaps at the tables of 6 run by the senior girls. You could end up anywhere, at the mercy of any year group. The table leader served the food from tureens and I guess this was meant to teach us the civilities of polite dining. I dreaded it.

The long journey by bus and, later, train; the name-taped uniform – some of it passed down from an older girl whose mother had her hair done by mine; outdoor and indoor shoes - it was unnerving new territory and set me apart from home and my sister.

My parents were so proud of me. I'd left the house on my first day all uniformed up with the badged beret and bright red three quarter length socks shining out as I walked down our street to the bus stop - a real leather satchel strapped to my back gleaming like a polished chestnut . But sitting in that first form classroom I felt very small. When they brought in the local Mayoress to teach us how to lose the northern accent and speak 'properly' in a few scheduled elocution lessons I felt smaller.

I'd always been drilled at home to speak 'correctly', not use slang and mind my grammar, but the accent had never been an issue. Flat vowels were never seen as something to improve on.

Although mum and dad were always impressed by anyone who had a 'lovely speaking voice' they saw themselves as working class and the accent was part of who they and we were. Suddenly, it was being implied at school that this wasn't good enough. Many of the prep girls were already well on the way to speaking posh, but for me a lengthened *a* in *path* and *bath* was excruciatingly artificial. I literally couldn't get my mouth around it. What was even worse, however, was the shame it sparked in me about the way my own family spoke. There was no attention paid to valuing your own accent and respecting the culture that came with it. It was something to be eradicated. So for all those of us who heard that message clearly, class prejudice kicked into gear. I only wish I'd been strong enough to reject it but I wasn't. I just found myself struggling to say the word *my*. At home it was always *mi* as in *mi mum/mi dad.* In school I aspired to use the full-on version which sounded pretentious and jumped-up. It went with the uniform, learning French, showering in communal nakedness. A world away from Chesterton Drive - dinnertime at 12, teatime at 5.30 after dad had changed out of his overalls and kids playing out on the streets until dark. The contrast was sharp.

In the end, my accent didn't change significantly until I started teaching in London, unconsciously imbibing elongated vowels on a daily basis. When it came to covering the subject of accent, dialect and prejudice with a class, centred on the important Schools' Council's 1971 publication *Language in Use*, shared respect for family language history was paramount and I drew on my own experience to convey the message. It's still the case that when I go back home to Worksop even now I experience the self-conscious twinge of sounding different and being categorised by it. My family tells me that my vowels start to flatten gently after a few days there and I'm sure they're right.

Back to the sixties. While I was wearing two hats in Worksop and Retford my sister, still at St Anne's, was expected to fail her 11+ and did. In 1964 the Cavendish secondary modern was nearing completion and my parents applied for her to be put on its waiting list, perhaps hoping a brand new school would give her a brand new start. She was therefore allocated an initial place at a secondary modern in the centre of town while she waited to be transferred. It proved disastrous. Her dread of maths in particular saw her fall victim to a male teacher with a crude repertoire of punishments. If pupils scored below 10 in a test, the girls had to write out the times-tables 20 times and the boys were caned. A missed lesson on how to use a compass saw her humiliated when her first efforts were held up, quite literally, to ridicule. Not surprisingly, she felt poorly quite often, was absent too often and fell behind quickly in her first year. She transferred in the Easter of 1965 but there was no brand new start for her. Her weakness in maths saw her placed in the lowest set of the streamed first year intake. There she found the other subjects pitched low, lost whatever motivation she had had and pretty much gave up on school. CSEs were the aspiration only for those considered able and so she left at 15 without taking one examination, convinced she was, and always would be, academically weak.

Looking back now at her school books, carefully saved by my mother, the English teacher in me sees talent that would have been recognised and developed in a good comprehensive school today. She had untapped potential that the secondary modern, as she experienced it, failed to develop. It was still, essentially, anchored in selection and division. And my parents, in their anxiety that she shouldn't see herself as inferior, continued to play down the importance of academic success, something which I know now my mother in particular must have it found very hard to do.

As for me, my detachment at the time from all this tells me a great deal about a self-centredness in myself which dominated those years of schooling. I was immersed in the world of Retford High School which I grew to love, while my sister was becoming an acute observer of our family lives during those years and can describe now in pin sharp detail incidents, people and places I've long forgotten.

The encouragement I received in the early years at the grammar school wasn't great, however. I couldn't make head or tail of French at first. I dreaded PE and the communal showers, and my love of English was sorely tested during the first two years. Most continuous writing pieces were ticked and marked out of 10 with maybe a spelling correction here and there. There was no such thing as constructive feedback. In one saved exercise book in which I'd written the required descriptive passage about a shop and added a mysterious secret cellar below there is nothing more than this as an evaluation:

You were told to describe one room not two.

So I guess what I had was stamina and determination, the product of primary school success, whereas my sister had diffidence and a readiness to throw in the towel...an alternative product of the same system.

Through those secondary school years we began to grow apart in every possible way. I had to do 'prep' every night and lug the satchel full of books to and from school. She didn't. I always seemed to be preparing for tests and meeting deadlines. She wasn't. I even started to sound different. Our wavelengths became so far apart we couldn't possibly tune into one another. And to compound it, we were encouraged to spend even more time apart in the school holidays when mum was working – me at my beloved Auntie Besse's where I helped out in her wool shop and went with her to visit Uncle Arthur at work in the rather grand furniture shop where he was head salesman; my sister at our grandparents' OAP bungalow where she was adored and protected, by my grandma especially.

The expectations of the grammar school encouraged me to value the middle class elements of my Conservative-voting aunt and uncle's lifestyle whilst my mum and dad – Labour, always - slogged away at making ends meet. My aunt was a good local business-woman. She combined a shrewd ability to make her corner shop pay with infinite patience when customers wanted to buy a bit of conversation therapy with their balls of wool. She employed a succession of assistants to cover the hours she didn't work herself and both they and her regular customers respected and loved her, as did I. She let me help out in school holidays and I enjoyed every bit of it. Fully-fashioned stockings, embroidery silks the colour of jewels and glass-fronted cabinets full of wool to be 'laid away' and bought 2 ounces at a time. She taught me to add up in my head and serve with courtesy.

In school holidays, she and I would go together to bank the shop's takings in town and sometimes take the train to the warehouse in Manchester to buy stock. The 'travellers' – salesmen who came into the shop to persuade her to buy their products – introduced me to another working world very different from my father's.

My uncle who had once run a locally well-known dance band, in which my father had played, now gave clarinet and saxophone lessons in their beautifully furnished but rarely used 'sitting room'. My dad, meanwhile, was still earning much needed extra cash playing in the resident band at a dinner-dance venue every Friday and Saturday night.

Politically, the divide between my home and my aunt and uncle's was clear. My dad had no time for their sympathies, seeing them as Tory-loving capitalists and probably resenting their comparative wealth. I understood how he felt but loved the comforts of their home and a lifestyle that was closer to that of many of the girls I was associating with at Retford. There was never any open debate between the two households. It was an unspoken class war perpetuated largely by the two men who didn't really like one another very much. The two sisters had different rivalries, again unspoken and no less significant, but family affection between the two women usually kept things running smoothly if sparks seemed likely to fly.

My sister and I spent less and less time together during those years – she was grandma's favourite and I was Auntie Besse's and we can remember being apart in those separate places the Friday night John F Kennedy was shot. Significantly, it was in our home on Kilton that I later heard seriously engaged conversation about this and its consequences. In our house, every day began with Jack De Manio on the Home Service bringing the outside world in and his voice always accompanied breakfast and preparations for school. My aunt and uncle didn't really engage with the bigger world outside their own and it was my mother I turned to for help with schoolwork and to test me in preparation for exams. which she did, unfailingly. I realise now that she relished the vicarious pleasure of studying with me and love her for it.

There are vivid memories my sister and I do share, however, which have served to bring us closer together as we grow older. Mum doing her ironing to whatever was on the radio and all of us laughing at Round the Horn and The Navy Lark during Sunday lunches. Dad's years spent in service as a young footman in London – a whole other story – meant that for this meal there was sometimes a bottle of red wine with the (rare) beef, water in glasses and no elbows on the table, ever. He had left working in service with an absolute loathing for the upper classes but with an enduring respect for quality, good manners and what a person could achieve on their own merits. His own schooling had been pretty basic but he told us, with a certain amount of self-congratulation, that when the second world war needed recruits he listened to what other men were giving as their educational alma maters as he stood in line for the RAF and creatively converted the name of his village school into a public-school sounding institution. He went on to become a navigator. His brother, Ambrose, made the RAF a career for life, achieving Squadron Leader status, but after the war my dad came home to a first marriage which ended in divorce and a return to the life he'd left behind.

We also remember, after years of rain-sodden caravan holidays on the east coast, the bliss of two weeks a year touring Devon and Cornwall in our first car, an old Ford, staying in a range of B and Bs and once spending the night sleeping in it in a town car park when money had to be squeezed a bit. Sunday day trips to York museum, Monsal Dale, the Blue John mines in Matlock. Ours was not a culturally impoverished life by any means, but my grammar school world-values essentially centred on having or acquiring social status and there was simply no connection between that world and Kilton estate. There were stronger links between it and my aunt and uncle's lifestyle. New furniture bought often; very smart clothes in rather grand wardrobes; a second home rented for a while in a village nearby.

I'm not proud of the materialistic aspirations I developed through those middle years at grammar school. I'd learned what it meant not to be middle class, and, in fairness, can't lay the blame on anyone but myself for the disloyalty I showed to the values I had been raised to respect. The fact that my father painstakingly hand painted and restored his newly bought second-hand and treasured maroon Vauxhall Cresta didn't compensate for the embarrassment I felt as a teenager at his having an old, unfashionable car. I preferred my uncle's brand new Jowett Javelin. The fact that my parents both did manual jobs and were not solicitors or doctors made me feel disappointed in them as I knew they were both clever people and felt they ought to have achieved more. The arrogance and lack of awareness implicit in these home truths still makes me squirm, especially when I look back and remember that the source of whatever creative talents I have ever had came from within the walls of home.

Mum and dad had turned our council house in Chesterton Drive into the country cottage he had painted on the wall in Bridge Terrace. He panelled every inch of it in Lincrusta and the lounge looked like the inside of an inn. Before the panelling went on, he lined all the walls with white paper and told us to draw whatever we wanted wherever we wanted. Joy. He attached wooden beams to the ceiling with hooks for ornaments inherited from the Milnes side of the family and a line of jugs and coronation mugs ran along the top of the pelmet he made. He used metallic strips to create leaded-light windows and the central light fittings, made for him by a friend, were his own design of a simplified fleur-de-lys in wood and brass. But these 'big lights' were rarely used in our house. Cosy little lamps in corners created the glow they were after. So home was a good place to come back to after a day at Retford and although he'd made me my own desk in my bedroom, fixed on a bracket to fold out when needed, it was in the lounge where I preferred to do my homework, background noise from the television not troubling me particularly. It was a far cry from the hushed old library at school where we did our 'prep' lessons.

Whilst I was finding my feet and absorbing the atmosphere, I was quite a subdued pupil in the first two years of grammar school and photographs from the time show me to be neatly turned out with hair set in rollers by mum on Sunday nights. Trudy was forming good friendships, some lifelong, with other children on our street, but I felt I was seen by them as a bit of an oddball. The uniform alone was standout strange. The three quarter length red socks of autumn gave way to bright red tights in winter and the beret which had to be worn at all times travelling to and from school became an embarrassment. The summer uniform dresses which my grandmother copied carefully from an approved pattern to save money were never as perfect to me as the ones bought from Losebys - the recommended clothiers in Retford - and they bore no relation to fashionable clothes for 1960s, Beatles-loving teenage girls either. Add a hockey stick to the mix and I didn't really fit comfortably into either location. In the third form I rebelled.

The most sought after accolade to be won at the end of an academic year was a Position (P) badge. To earn it a girl had to be polite, punctual, wear immaculate uniform, work hard and make no waves. I wanted one so badly and can remember the joy of hearing my name read out at the end of my second year. I started the third year full of confidence. I was no longer phased by having to be a floater at lunchtime and knew all the ropes. I'd found my feet, was loving school and flexing muscles. New and interesting male teachers had joined the previously all-female staff – the best ones for me being two English teachers and the head of music. I sang in the choir and performed in plays: God in 'Noah's Fludde' and a rustic dancing girl in something else, shown to parents over a few nights as a double bill. My mother had to chisel off the remains of God's spirit-gummed beard every night and I can still smell the brown stain I had to be painted in to transform into a sun-tanned peasant underneath his flowing robes. But I loved it all and felt I was back in the comfort zone of St Anne's.

This proved to be an unfortunate development as complacency took hold. School rules seemed less important now, punctuality didn't matter and the Sunday night shampoo and set was no more as I rejected the neatly curled hairstyle in favour of a Cilla Black/Mary Quant cut attempted unhappily by my mother. Puberty had set in and I went off the rails.

I was regularly cheeky to the Latin master who struggled to control our class and was sent to stand outside the classroom on more than one occasion. I started to accrue 'slips' –the punishment marks which led to deducted house points. I thought the slightly spicy folk club for older girls run on Friday lunchtimes by the handsome English teacher was the height of social success and prep fell by the wayside. Academic achievement plummeted and I found myself at a Saturday session for those failing an end of term Geography exam for which I had not bothered to revise. When the P badge was ceremoniously removed from me in the final assembly of that year it was the public stamp of disapproval, but what really cut through was the articulate dressing down dealt out to me in front of my class by the other respected English teacher when he had had enough of my behaviour. I stepped right back in line. Rebellion over.

From then on, my days at Retford were largely happy and marked by success, academically and socially. My love of English was nourished by the two subject teachers who moved a distance away from the parsing of sentences into the wonderful realms of discussing literature and responding to writing with encouraging intervention. A real awakening. Overall, I survived the awkward years of snobbery and bad judgements and stayed well and truly grounded through a succession of Saturday jobs which my parents felt I should take to supplement the 10 shillings pocket money I received from dad on Fridays. How wise they were.

They began with an embarrassing spell on a Worksop market stall selling old-fashioned women's underwear. Bloomers, basically, pegged up in a washing line arrangement behind which I hid from anyone who might know me. My maternal granddad had secured this opportunity for me as he worked there himself, setting up the stalls, and had 'connections'. For seven shillings and sixpence a day I joined the world of work. Other jobs followed, including a spell in the salon where my mother worked. The owner quickly realised I could do more than wash hair and dry towels and I found myself seated at the cash desk at the end of the day, adding up all the charges hand written on the till roll and counting the cash. If it didn't tally I didn't go home. £1 a day. When I moved into shop work it was heaven. Timothy Whites - an old-fashioned chemist's shop where I had to sell medical products I'd never heard of and weigh out loose soap flakes. This later became the first brightly lit store to open in the new shopping precinct, built where Bridge Terrace once stood. The workings of the fickle finger of fate weren't lost on me but I loved working there anyway.

These jobs taught me life skills. The men and women I worked alongside gently teased me, told me dodgy jokes and – in once case- bullied me, but each job moved me on and away from complacency, snobbery and back towards respect for everything my parents had done for me throughout their own hard-working lives.

Back at school, all my end of year exams had gone well except for Latin, still taught by my bête noir, and I'd been entered a year early for O level English Language and Maths, but when my English teachers said they thought I should be thinking about staying on in the sixth form and applying to university it came as a complete jolt. University had never been considered at all in our house, or even at my aunt and uncle's. My father thought I should aspire to become a secretary, maybe a bilingual one if the French held up. That would make him very proud. He couldn't see the point of staying on to do A levels when I could get a good job before getting married. This was compounded by my Headmistress's reaction in my fairly limited 'career' interview when I tentatively shared my intentions. Her raised eyebrow was followed by another of her killer lines: "It's always commendable to aim high".

Back at home, my mother stepped in. The 12 year age-gap between my parents counted for something. She argued for another two years of schooling and, yes, maybe a try for university. In our road, if you weren't 'courting' or engaged by the age of 18 something was definitely up and I respect her so much for countering all the questions from neighbours about my romantic prospects with her support for education first. I suspect now she was actually hoping I'd stay close to home and eventually marry the boyfriend I had at the time who was 4 years older, had a good job as a fitter and whose parents they had befriended but she stood by me and I headed off into the sixth form.

By April 1968, I was preparing studiously for final A level exams and had a conditional place at university. At the same time, my sister was leaving school for good at the age of 15, to take up a job in a delicatessen in town. She had no doubts it was what she wanted to do and no-one was persuading her otherwise. It was the natural conclusion of schooling which had done little if anything to build her confidence or self-belief. She would have nothing more to do with formal education. There would be no picking up the pieces later on in life – no 'lifelong learning' policies would motivate her to go back, to put herself at risk. Looking back now, she summarises her memories of her schooldays very simply: she hated them.

Without being disloyal to the school I grew to love and the good teachers who sent me on my way to a lifestyle considered at the time a successful outcome for a girl from a council estate, when I hear today's politicians still promoting a grammar school education for the elevation of the 'disadvantaged ' working class child, I see red. My 1960's grammar school education was not an antidote to class prejudice. Quite the opposite. It didn't recognise or teach me to value and respect my own cultural background or the strengths of my gender. I look back on my years there with great affection for its smallness, its public-school style traditions and the good friendships I made but I can't say that it sent me out of its doors empowered to stand as an equal with all others. In this respect, my own children left their comprehensive school far better prepared for whatever came next.

In 1968 I went straight from school to a 'plate-glass' university in Lancaster and initially, to some extent, history repeated itself. I had good A level grades and a love of the subjects but I found myself at first staying silent in seminars where boys seemed more at ease and girls who had been at co-ed schools coped far better. The doubts about my abilities resurfaced, just as they had in the first form at Retford. Imposter syndrome. But it turned out I'd joined a university which actively promoted what we now call inclusivity and during that first year I met students from the widest range of conventional and non-conventional educational backgrounds. They were not all 18 and fresh from grammar or public schools. Many were much older with pretty wild pasts, some were being sponsored by employers, others came from backgrounds like my own. There was an openness, acceptance and generosity at university that gave me the environment I needed to strike the balance I needed and although I never really went home again I felt I could get back in tune with everything it held.

Reading this through with me, my sister has been as surprised to learn about the struggles I had through some of those school years as I have been to unearth them again so easily. It's been therapeutic for us both to talk openly about errors of judgement our parents made with the best of loving intentions and to re-visit childhood experiences with candour. Am I a successful product of selective schooling and social engineering? I suppose I am. Is my sister a victim of it? Most definitely, yes. In the end, however, no matter what divided us and set us on different paths, the early family life we shared has proved stronger and has enabled us now to come back together when it really matters. Even better: our mother has lived to witness it.

Chapter 3

Tambourines to Tolstoy

Margaret Peacock

It was at the beginning of the Autumn Term of the Upper Sixth that Miss Leonard, the Headmistress of my grammar school, Wisbech High School for Girls, called me to her study for the 'destination' interview she had with all the girls. When I entered she was sitting behind her desk, in the black gown worn by all the mistresses, with her usual expression – severe even when she was smiling. But I wasn't worried; I was getting good marks in my A levels.

"Ah, Margaret, come in and sit down. Now tell me, what are you thinking of doing next?"

"My parents would like me to go to university," I said. Maybe I thought it would carry more weight than just saying 'I would like…'

How wrong could I be? The response was immediate and certain, accompanied by a look which was part serious, part sympathetic.

"My dear," she said, leaning over her desk towards me, "sometimes we know better than our parents. Girls from your class don't stand the pace at university. Much better to think of something else. What about a secretarial course?"

I remember the shock. This was 1964, twenty years after the Butler Education Act. The grammar school system was *supposed* to provide opportunities for clever working class children to enter the professions and my parents and I had bought into this wholesale. Clearly, however, as far as Wisbech

High School was concerned, 'opportunities' didn't extend as far as university; that was still the domain of the middle class.

I think I was more conscious of my parents' disappointment than my own, at least to start with. They didn't have anything against secretarial work – it was a step up from the agricultural work they had done all their lives – but it wasn't the entry into the professions they had envisaged for me. And this was a view vociferously supported by my mum's sister, Nellie, who had been a secretary and now taught shorthand and typing in the town; she also had different ambitions for her niece – she knew the weight of 'letters after your name'.

Bizarrely, considering that I'd always been fairly rebellious, I accepted Miss Leonard's advice. Maybe deep down I'd always felt I didn't quite fit into that middle class world and this was the proof.

Years later, when I eventually did get a degree, my mother advertised it in the local paper, hoping that Miss Leonard would see it and regret her words.

****

My father came from northern Salvation Army stock. His father had been a miner in Ashington, near Newcastle, and, like all the miners' families, had suffered severe privations in the 1926 General Strike. I used to listen with rapt attention when my father told me how he went to school without shoes. Once, though, my mother, interrupting one of the stories about how little they had to eat, said, "What on earth is he telling you? Your grandmother *ran* the Salvation Army soup kitchen in Ashington and she'll have made sure they had enough to eat!"

Exaggerated or not, these stories prompted a romantic fascination with the mining community, further influenced later by D. H. Lawrence, and I wish I'd talked more to my grandfather about it. In my twenties, on a trip north, I went to Ashington and saw where he had grown up - the small, back to back house, with a single track railway line running between the houses for the free coal.

I don't know how militant grandad was, if at all, but soon after the strike, he brought the family south and, for some reason, ended up at Wisbech. The family comprised my father, his older brother George and his sisters, Hilda and Rose. My dad was 16 and he started working in the fish and chip shop which my grandfather kept, presumably on some sort of lease. Fish and chips remained a weakness all his life and were at least partly responsible for his later portliness!

The family must have been Salvationists from its early days, and my grandmother, who died when I was about 2, was known as a real Sally Army tartar. She ruled the family with a rod of iron, and wouldn't allow any such devil-made frivolities as cinemas or football matches, which my father had to sneak off and go to secretly. Alcohol and smoking were, of course, forbidden, as was swearing in any form – 'bloody' meant the 'blood of Christ', I was told, and was blasphemy. When I was born, and my mother said they were calling me 'Margaret Sandra', grandma apparently said, "Sandra? You can't call her that – it's an *actress's* name!" And it couldn't get much worse than that, to her. But my mother obviously stuck to her guns, because that is, indeed, my middle name.

My mother joined the Salvation Army when she married my father. She had recently returned to Wisbech after living in London with an aunt where she had been sent when her mother died, orphaning her at 14. Her father had been killed at Ypres in 1916. Back in Wisbech, to live with her grandparents, she was put into service to earn her keep. The story went that one Sunday, her day off, she and her friend Edie were walking around, with nothing much to do, when they decided to go into the Salvation Army hall 'for a laugh'. That laugh altered their lives for good. They met my dad and his brother George. Romance blossomed and some time after my mother, Doris, married Les, and Edie married George. My mother was 19 and my dad was 18.

Tragedy, however, was to beset my parents' lives. My brother Gerald, born in the first year of their marriage, was given a much coveted bicycle for his sixth birthday. On his first trip out, with a friend on the back, the bicycle was hit by a passing car. He died at the hospital. I can only imagine the depth of my parents' grief, but I know that soon after they moved to Yaxley, near Peterborough, because to stay risked my mother's life. So my father took a job in the Peterborough brick works, where, in my mother's words, the unbearable heat nearly killed him. When he heard, therefore, that a farmer of a nearby milk farm needed hands, he went along. Asked if he could milk a cow, he thought, 'can't be difficult', so he said yes. Some time later, after pulling at the poor cow's teats to no avail, he had to admit it was his first time. The farmer saw the funny side and gave him the job. It was the beginning of a life on farms, which he loved.

I was born ten years after Gerald's death, a miracle baby I suppose, after the years of mourning and then the war, in which my dad was a dispatch rider in the Home Guard, farming being a protected occupation. These were the years of Atlee's Labour government and the beginning of the NHS, which was apparently rebelliously challenged by Wisbech doctors. My father probably agreed – he was a staunch 'Churchillian', even reading books about the war years, though not a great reader of anything else apart from The Sketch, the only newspaper I ever saw in our house. Later, he was vitriolic about Harold Wilson and Arthur Scargill; in some ways a typical working class Tory but in other ways liberal – he hated, for instance, the local racial prejudice against the travellers who came to the area to pick the fruit and was very generous and kind to the farm workers who were pitifully low paid.

By the time I was born they had moved back to Wisbech, and my first memory is of sitting on a carpet in a modern bungalow, watching 'Hank' on a very early television. I must have been about three so it was 1949.

My parents had fallen on their feet at that point in their lives. My father was the sleeping partner in a horticultural company, managing the day to day work while the other partner managed the business. Perhaps inevitably, the bubble burst. My dad discovered that the other partner had been gambling away all the profits and bankrupted the firm. No company, no job, no bungalow, overnight.

Cherry Tree Cottage, our next tied house, in Clenchwarton, near King's Lynn, was a typical yellow brick double-fronted Fens house. It was very near a railway line which took us, every Saturday, into King's Lynn on a wonderful steam train whose musty smell I can still recall. There we used to buy the post-war stipulated cod liver oil and malt which I considered 'toffee' and ate with relish. Sweets, of course, were still rationed.

My father was the foreman on a fruit farm and money clearly didn't run to a car. We cycled everywhere, but the journey I remember most was the arduous Sunday routine to the A47 main road to Wisbech. At the end of the very long lane, we left our bikes in the yard, ironically, of a pub, and caught the bus to the Army. We did this trip, regardless of weather, with mum in her bonnet and me on the back of her bicycle until I was big enough to ride my own. The only Sunday we missed, I think, was in 1953 when floods wreaked havoc in Norfolk and my dad was trapped overnight in the Odeon in King's Lynn with my aunt and uncle and no telephone to inform my frantic mother.

Sundays were always the same. Sunday School for mum and me at 10.00 a.m., while my dad played his trombone at the 'Open Air' meeting in the Marketplace. Then it was a meeting from 11.00 to 12.00, lunch and back for Sunday School again and another meeting – a more jolly affair than the morning service, with lots of music, singing, clapping and tambourines with streamers coloured red, blue and yellow, the Army colours. William Booth famously said, 'Why should the devil have all the best tunes', and many Army songs (not hymns) are very cheerful; I even remember a chorus called 'I love the Army rock and roll', which made me and the other young people cringe!

The Army was like a family. Every woman was an 'aunt' to me, and every man an 'uncle'. Some of them, of course, were my real relatives – as well as grandad and Aunt Alice (whom he married after grandma died – with me as bridesmaid, wearing a blue velvet dress and pink rosebuds in my hair....), there were the Peacock aunts and uncles and cousins, all of whom wore the uniform, played in the Band and sang in the Songsters. Grandad, like my dad, played trombone. Only one of my mother's three sisters was in the army – her oldest sister, Nellie, whose real name was Helena, but who had been forced to change it on entering service, because 'Helena is not a servant's name'. Aunt Nellie had been a Salvation Army officer, in Manchester, in the 30s, looking after 'unmarried mothers'. She mellowed as she grew older, but I remember her as pretty stern in my childhood.

The army was a way of life which engaged us in some way or another most of the time – weekly practices (Band, Songsters, Singing Company – the junior choir, for which I played the piano), Harvest Festivals, Sales of Work, visiting Bands and Songster Brigades who were billeted with us all, Youth Clubs, Girls Guides and Scouts, summer camps. Two highlights of the year for children were the Sunday School Anniversary, when children dressed up, performed ('recitations', solos and duets on instruments being learned), and were awarded books with moral stories, and the outing to Hunstanton, the nearest seaside resort. For the Army 'insiders', this was a jamboree – all the people in that extended family off for a paddle, a donkey ride, candy-floss, ice cream, deck chairs on the beach and fish and chips in the 'Kit Kat', an Art Deco restaurant on the front, before piling back into the coach.

Given the centrality of the Salvation Army to our lives, religion itself strangely played a very small part. We didn't say grace at meal-times and apart from my nightly 'Gentle Jesus' prayer, the only times I remember people praying in our house was when the corps officer – the Major, or the Captain, or whoever was stationed in Wisbech at the time, would visit, and it was always slightly embarrassing.

I started primary school at Clenchwarton. The school, which still exists, was a long, low Victorian building, comprising one room which they separated into classrooms with corrugated wooden dividers. In the winter it was freezing cold, heated only by a pot-bellied stove, next to which the teachers used to de-freeze the free 1/3 pint of milk famously cut by Margaret Thatcher. I wouldn't have minded that – I hated the milk!

With more than one eye on the future, my mother had taught me to read and write before I went to school, using the 'Janet and John' books, and the 'Beacon Readers' which I still have. Though only educated up to the age of 14, mum's own spelling and grammar were perfect and she read a lot, romances and the monthly Readers' Digest books. As an only child in the middle of the Norfolk countryside reading was my main occupation; Enid Blyton's 'Noddy' books, which we bought on our trips to King's Lynn, were a great favourite, as were A.A. Milne's 'Pooh' books. And every week, there were comics – Bunty, The Beano and The Dandy (also read by my dad), and later, School Friend and Girls' Crystal. There was no television but we listened to the radio - 'Listen with Mother' with Daphne Oxenford, and 'Children's Hour' which featured 'Toy Town', with Larry the Lamb and Mr. Mayor - as we toasted crumpets on the open fire. The idylls of memory – maybe.

I loved Clenchwarton School. The Brer Rabbit stories we were read on Friday afternoons; drawing the patterns of snowflakes which landed on the windows when it snowed; nature study walks in the summer; my best friend, Catherine Elcombe. It was a happy time, except for one sadness, when a Romany friend called Esther, who had taken me to meet her parents in their brightly coloured caravan, died of diphtheria, which had not been eradicated yet. I was devastated.

When I was seven, we moved back to Wisbech, where dad had got a job managing a big fruit farm owned by old-style landed gentry. The house, another typically Fenland double fronted house in the middle of nowhere, was even more primitive than Cherry Tree Cottage. It had no running water, electricity or bathroom when we moved in. My dad used to pull water from a well outside the back door, and we lit the rooms with Aladdin and Tilley lamps which gave off a pleasant mellow light. The toilet was outside and the only heating was by open fires downstairs. But it was a roomy house and my dad soon tamed the garden and grew our vegetables and his beloved flowers – wonderful sweet peas and chrysanthemums which he sometimes 'showed'.

The next question and one which caused a huge stir, was where I was to go to school.

Cambridgeshire Education Authority allocated me a place at a village school which I would get to by cycling along our lane and crossing a busy road. My mother was having none of it. She had lost one child to an accident with a car and a bike; she was not going to lose another. So she appealed. She wanted me to go to Peckover School, in Wisbech, because I could get the bus at the end of the road and not cross any main roads.

The local authority refused the appeal. But my mother, normally mild, became a tiger. She wrote to the local M.P., Major Legge-Burke, and asked him to fight her case. He did.

The case was heard 'in Parliament', as my mother proudly put it and she won! Peckover School had to offer me a place.

While all this was going on (several months) I was educated at home as best as my parents could. They bought a set of Arthur Mee's Children's Encyclopedias and W. H. Smiths provided work books – English, Maths and lots of verbal and non-verbal exercises and puzzles which, in the fullness of time stood me in very good stead for the 11+, though they can't have known that. And, of course, I read and read, moving on to The Secret Seven, The Famous Five and the Malory Towers books.

The day came when I started at Peckover Junior School but instead of this being a joyful experience, it was a sour one. The headmaster, Mr. Petch, clearly furious at being instructed to take this pupil, presumably over his numbers, showed his anger – to an eight year old girl! I don't think he spoke a civil word to me in the three years I was there.

By the time we reached our final year, the importance of the 11+ had been carefully drummed into us by Mr. Binley, our teacher, and we spent most of that year preparing for it. There was no doubt in our minds that our secondary school - the Girls' High School, the Boys' Grammar School or the secondary modern, the Queen's School – would determine the rest of our lives. My parents, of course, were very keen that I pass.

And not only did I pass, but I was offered a scholarship to go to Wymondham College, a successful boarding grammar school in South Norfolk. That posed a dilemma. My parents were obviously as proud as punch that I'd been so successful and knew that this would be a great opportunity for me – a farm worker's daughter mixing with the toffs. And part of me wanted to go (Malory Towers …..) But I also knew that it would be very hard for my mother; the ghost of Gerald was ever present. So I decided to take my chances with Wisbech High School.

Though I was only pupil in the school to have 'passed straight through' the 11+, Mr. Petch, presumably livid, continued to ignore me and only Mr. Binley congratulated me. And it was Mr. Binley who came up with an idea to keep me busy while the others, who had to retake in some weeks' time, had to get down to more and more practice. He suggested I write stories and make them into little books. I thought this was a great idea, and set to writing mystery stories imitating my adored Enid Blyton. I think I still have one of the books – the 'Mystery of the Old House' or some such.

Wisbech High School was (and still is, though now much expanded) housed in a big Georgian house on the banks of the River Nene. It had been established in 1905 by the liberal Quaker Peckover family to complement the boys' school across the river. Until the 1944 Education Act, both schools had been fee-paying, with a number of scholarships for the clever poor, but were now 'enjoying' a foray into the state system. (In the 1960s, they both reverted to the private sector rather than become comprehensive.)

At the traditional pre-starting parents' meeting, Miss Leonard laid down the rules that High School 'gels' must obey. Standing on the platform of the wood panelled hall which doubled as a gym, her grey hair pulled back in her customary bun, she told us her expectations. She must have talked about working hard, but what I remember was the emphasis on the uniform. Our gymslips must touch the floor when we knelt; berets were not to be perched on the backs of backcombed hair; we must have outside and inside shoes and, bizarrely, white airtex knickers had to be worn beneath our regulation navy blue ones. No rationale, no explanation, but the impression that this somehow encompassed the spirit of the new sphere into which we were moving.

The 40 girls in each year group were strictly streamed into two bands. I was in the A band, but most of the other working class girls, many of whom were bussed in from outlying villages, were in the B band. The girls from professional families, whose parents had been to university and knew teachers socially, were mainly in the A band – destined to follow their parents into medicine, teaching, law or business. I realize now that they were the girls who would have gone to the school when it was fee-paying; they were now getting a free pass for a while.

Nowadays, we talk a lot about the 'culture' of a school, and its impact on student achievement. I'm pretty sure there was no such discussion in the 50s; the culture was certain, coherent and confident. Assemblies were Christian – a prayer, a hymn and a 'talk' from the head – and patriotism was entrenched. We sang Jerusalem, of course, and our school hymn, 'Dear Lord and Father of Mankind', but also the brazenly patriotic 'All men must be free' to Elgar's Pomp and Circumstance March, when we sang how 'Brutes and braggarts' might 'have their little day' but 'We would never bow the knee'. No shame about colonialism there!

The school unashamedly and explicitly set out to 'gentrify' those of us who had what they saw as unacceptable plebeian habits. I remember Miss Leonard, one day during lunch, bending over a girl near to me and showing her, in her shrill voice, how to use a knife, which she had been holding like a pen. "Finger on top, so you slice (demonstrated) and shove (demonstrated)." The girl was so embarrassed and I was glad that day that I had got that right at least.

Elocution lessons set out to eliminate the Fenland accent. At home, I don't remember my parents using Norfolk or Cambridgeshire dialect words, but they certainly did have the accent, in my father's case mixed with his native Geordie – always a short 'a' in 'castle'. The elocution teacher emphasised the need to separate each word clearly, not lazily missing out, for example, the 't' in 'wa'er'. For some reason I remember the rhyme we intoned day after day:

'There was a boy whose name was Jim;

His friends were very good to him (to...him...not 'toim')

They gave him tea and toast and jam

And slices of delicious ham.' (emphasis on the 'delicious')

Latin was ostensibly the divider of the two bands, but so were expectations. As we got older, the school's purpose in providing the different strata of the workforce became clearer: the A band girls were being prepared for university; the B band girls weren't – they took fewer O levels and not many entered the Sixth Form, rather taking up local retail jobs, or secretarial work. Miss Leonard obviously thought I was more naturally a candidate for that band and had had to tolerate me and a few others like me in the more middle class A band. In retrospect this would seem to contradict the whole reason for allowing working class children into the grammar schools and smacks of a lack of communication to the head teachers!

My parents were as supportive as they could be. My dad would test me nightly on Latin conjugations and French verbs, and attempt to check my maths homework, taking great pride in all the difficult stuff his daughter was learning, though he must have simultaneously been aware of the potential for this to drive a wedge between us. They never missed a parents' evening, though I think they found them a bit of an ordeal, being quite in awe of the mistresses who seemed to come from a different world with their plummy accents and chalky gowns. One day, though, they got the opportunity to make closer acquaintance with one of them. One Science lesson in the First Form, the Science teacher (and also my form mistress), Miss Smith, dangled a skeleton in front of us, and I fainted! Miss Smith took me home in her car and had a good old laugh about it with my dad – who gave her a box of strawberries to take home and made a friend for life.

English I loved from the beginning. Mrs. Roberts, my inspirational teacher right through to A level, introduced us systematically to the classics, reading aloud 'around the class': 'Moonfleet', 'David Copperfield', 'Oliver Twist' and Shakespeare – 'A Midsummer Night's Dream' first, followed by Henry V, with, as an end of term treat, the Lawrence Olivier film. Apart from that, English was comprehension and grammar exercises – parsing and précis which I actually enjoyed and which have stood me in very good stead, especially when I became an English teacher myself. I loved it all.

There was no such subject as 'drama' on the curriculum, but we did have an annual drama festival of one-act plays on the school's picturesque open air theatre. It was great fun. I remember being in 'The Bishop's Candlesticks', a play set in the kitchens of the 'Macbeths' castle, and an adaptation of 'Romeo and Juliet' when I played Juliet dressed in a blue silk counterpane from my mother's bed. I remember Mrs. Roberts explaining the sexual connotations in the 'Gallop apace, you fiery-footed steeds' speech to me – to my great embarrassment! And we did choral speaking, too, at the local cinema, with Miss Salt, the music teacher, on the stage conducting the whole school in 'The Smugglers' Song' and Christopher Fry's 'Boy with a Cart'.

I find the recent revival of what they now call 'knowledge teaching' a little sad and not a little misconceived. At the time I didn't question the school's teaching methods – learning from text books and regurgitating facts – but I'd be hard put to remember much of it now. It wasn't until A level that we were encouraged to understand anything in depth, and even then, independent thought wasn't really encouraged.

Never very sporty, I hated the hockey we played on muddy or frozen pitches in the winter though the middle class girls seemed to thrive on it. Summer was better – I was quite good at tennis and even made the school team in the 4th form. But summer or winter, the Scottish Head of Games, Miss Prentice, oversaw compulsory showering. If we didn't manage to undress in one minute and get dressed in two minutes, we were sent 'round the hockey pitch' whatever the weather. I think it was meant to teach us discipline, but I think the only thing it taught me was how power can be misused (not a bad lesson for a future head teacher).

Miss Prentice's other obsession was Scottish dancing which we practised all year round so that we were ready for Sports Day when the whole school 'Marched On' in height order, from our hiding place in the school copse, out onto the field. There, we separated into two lines which formed the boundary for the final of the 800 yards race. Then, after all the races were done (I was only ever in the finals of the obstacle and slow bicycle races) came our dancing display– newly choreographed each year and pictured in the local press. I can still remember some of the steps.

Although I loved school, and never missed a day, I was not a particularly well behaved student. I was a 'chatterbox' and I liked pranks – like putting the wastepaper basket where poor dumpy, well-meaning Miss Smith would fall over it as she reached to the furthest side of the blackboard to write out maths equations. But my cardinal sin was that I questioned too much, perhaps in line with the new sense of rebellion in the world, perhaps because I was naturally insubordinate, but whatever the reason, I spent quite a lot of time standing outside classrooms, especially Science. However, I still managed to get 13 O levels, including a couple in the Sixth form.

In my teens, perhaps inevitably, tensions grew between the two strands of my life – the Salvation Army and the life I increasingly wanted to live with my High School friends. My two closest friends were Babs and Jen. Babs was also from the agricultural working class and in the B band; Jen, whose family were lower middle class, was in my class. We played records in each others' bedrooms (Ben E King; the Everly Brothers, Elvis), met in coffee bars in town and went on holiday together – a caravan park at Yarmouth with Babs and a North Wales boarding house with Jen – and built a social life which was bound to cause friction at home for me. In the summer months, there were Friday night dances held by the foreign students who came to the area for fruit-picking, and it was only with great reluctance and after heated argument that I was allowed to go – in the clothes which my father thought made me look like 'something off the streets' – tight skirt or one with masses of starched petticoats, stiletto heels in gunmetal grey, back-combed hair and lots of makeup – the fashion of the late 50's rock and roll years. In retrospect, my dad was probably right, but at the time we thought we looked great!

I'm not sure when I became conscious of class divisions, at school or in society. In the agricultural working class world, my dad's manager status and possibly their religion, set them apart from the farm workers, even though my mother plucked apples, picked strawberries and harvested potatoes with them. They were 'respectable' though not rich, and it was possibly that which gave me the confidence to make friends with the middle class girls – the doctor's daughter who had a swimming pool in their back garden, the local pharmacists' daughter, Mr. Binley's daughter. But there were times when the differences showed. I remember, for example, the day I invited a group of the girls home to tea, without telling my mother. In my enthusiasm to ingratiate myself with them, the impact on her hadn't occurred to me. 'Tea' for us was not a snack but the main meal of the day, a hot meal eaten when my dad finished work, and my mother, still in her work clothes, was understandably horrified when I arrived home with four new posh 'friends'. But probably realising that this was important to me, she rose to the occasion and managed something – I don't remember exactly what but she probably added sausages to the pork chops, made more potatoes and had something different herself. The girls thought it was marvellous – proper food at 5 o' clock! What I remember also about that day, though, was that when we reached my house on our bikes, one of them said, "Oh, you live in a big house!" – clearly expecting something very different.

As time went on, it became clear to me that we were poorer than these new friends. Unlike them, I had a Saturday job – serving in Shawl's bakery for 15s a day, and when a French exchange was offered in the 4th form, my parents had to swallow their pride and ask the school for help, though I'm sure I covered this up, embarrassed for them as much as for myself.

The 'going out' fight had pretty much been won by the time we were in the Sixth Form, and also our new tastes were more acceptable to my father. It was 1962 and we saw ourselves as becoming much more 'cultured'. We moved on from Elvis to the Beatles (who we saw at Peterborough Odeon before they were top of the bill) and started going to a jazz club and drinking gin and lime. Our clothes changed to jeans and roll neck black jumpers and we started to visit bookshops and art galleries and go on school trips to the Cambridge Arts Theatre. And our taste in food started to change; we would buy little bottles of olive oil from the chemists' and put it on our salad, much to our mothers' amusement, and we would cook Vesta Chow Mein or Chicken Curry for our Saturday tea. Consciously or unconsciously, everything was broadening the gap between my parents and me.

The tensions between this life and that of the Army were bound to blow up at some point. The crunch came when pressure was put on me to become a full member of the Salvation Army. This would mean wearing the uniform and signing the pledge. I couldn't do it. I could no longer blindly accept the Christian beliefs I was brought up with; I had begun to question everything, including the existence of God. It must have hurt my parents but they didn't make a fuss; they realised I think that this was the price of the social mobility they wanted. They probably thought I would return at some point, though that never did happen.

World events were contributing to my changing views too. The Cuban crisis happened when I was in the Lower Sixth. We were all at a Sixth Form conference that day, ironically entitled 'Is Christianity dead?' and at the time appointed for the Russian ships to turn around, a boy stood up and demanded that the conference be halted, saying, "We might never get home today – we might all be dead from a nuclear bomb!" Obviously an exaggeration, but that was how frightened we all were. The morality of CND had become more relevant than the old morality of religion, though I personally didn't become politically active until much later, when I had left home and lived in London.

Taking Miss Leonard's advice, after the Sixth Form and a stay in France as an au pair to improve my spoken French, I started a bilingual secretarial course at the French Lycée in South Kensington. At the end of the first year, I was called to another interview, with another head teacher.

After welcoming me and inviting me to sit down, the Principal said, "Margaret, why are you here?"

Here we go again, I thought.

"Because I want to be a bilingual secretary," I replied, puzzled.

But I was in for another shock. "No you don't," said Mademoiselle. "You will never be satisfied with being someone's secretary; you will always want to be the boss. You should be at an English university, reading English literature, because that is what you love."

Did her astuteness come from not being steeped in the English class system like Miss Leonard? Vive egalité, fraternité and liberté!

I took her advice too, and never looked back.

******

After my English degree and PGCE, I made a conscious decision to teach in comprehensive schools and eventually became the head teacher of one. I never looked back with anything resembling longing at my grammar school, and I never tried to emulate anything about it, even though I have to admit that in the end it had worked out well for me. I had by this time become politically aware and wanted to be part of a different process, one which could really lead to success for anyone, regardless of background. So as Head of English in Kidbrooke, the first purpose-built comprehensive in Greenwich and then as head teacher of Chestnut Grove school in Balham, South London, I set out to do all I could to ensure high expectations and achievement for all, regardless of class, ethnicity, gender.

Barriers to this ambition, of course, existed and still exist, particularly in the continuing survival of the public school system, and the 'who you know' and 'what school you went to' culture which pervades some professions. I don't deceive myself that we've reached a stage when we have real and consistent meritocracy or social mobility; unbelievably, poverty remains, even in this country, the greatest determinant of a child's educational progress and destination, so there must be huge numbers of bright, poor children left behind even now. At least in the comprehensive structure, however, all have a fighting chance, and though not perfect, it's the best we have and I'm glad to have played a part in its development over the years.

So how successful was this stepping stone towards post war meritocracy? Did Miss Leonard and all her peers across the country move a generation of working class children into the middle class? The answer is probably yes, a few (but only a few) and yes, a partial 'success'. But it seems to me that it would be more accurate to say that a new class was created – one with roots in the working class together with the professional confidence which comes from higher education. These were the people who, like me, became militants in the various struggles for equality of opportunity in education through the decades since the 1950s – and I'm glad I was able to play a small part in that process.

Chapter 4

The '60s Meritocracy – MINO

Paul Davies

"So what do you do at university?" my Aunty May asked.

"Well – I read quite a lot and I write quite a lot and I discuss quite a lot," I said.

"Yes, I know that," she replied, "but what do you actually do?"

For many years that exchange with my great aunt typified for me the distance between me and my parents and their parents' generation, as did her remark when she was offered a mango. She was adamant that she didn't want any of that foreign muck; she'd have a banana.

That gulf was essentially a result of what we were assured was the development of a meritocracy in Britain in the '60s. And at the time I bought into that only to realise later – and painfully – that it was, to use a useful acronym – MINO. Meritocracy in Name Only.

That isn't quite fair.

My life is very different from my older relatives' lives. Despite the terrible environment of my teens, I passed my A Levels, went to university, got my PhD, and eventually earned a fair amount of money. Despite all that, however, I still feel very much like Jude the Obscure, on the outside looking in. I had been told in my early teens what a meritocracy was and that we had one, and been told how important social mobility was – but then the reality was so different. At the time I thought it was because I didn't see things clearly. Later I realised that I had seen through MINO. It was quite devastating.

MINO has made me feel a failure all my life.

It doesn't keep me awake at night. It did make me determined for my children.

Those early claims for the meritocracy's arrival were at best premature. And for me, who had believed what I was told, pernicious. My whole understanding of meritocracy was fatally flawed because I had been brought up to look at it in the wrong way entirely, as I think nearly all working class children were.

It was, perhaps deliberately, confused with social mobility.

So how does that happen?

First my personal background and then my personal experience of surviving that maelstrom – highly individual perhaps – and my slow progress in learning that whatever was developing in our society in the '60s and beyond was not in any real sense a meritocracy.

My Background

My parents, both eleven when the war broke out, were married at 18 while my father was doing National Service. He was invalided home from Berlin in 1947 suffering from tuberculosis and they were desperately poor with my mother pawning her wedding ring while he was in the sanatorium. I don't remember ever going hungry after I was born in 1949, but I knew we were poor – shamefully poor it felt to me although I think my five year old self must have exaggerated that. I do know that in my first year at Hearnville School, we created a calendar and we were asked to bring a penny from home to pay for the little printed months and days of the year that we had to attach to it. I was too frightened to ask for that penny at home, and was so embarrassed in class. I never was able to finish the calendar.

My mother was a bright girl, eldest of five at the time war broke out. She had gained a scholarship to a selective school but she was evacuated to Bury St Edmunds and so was never able to take up the scholarship. She was then summoned home at the age of twelve to look after her siblings when her mother had a nervous breakdown.

My grandfather was a printer and on the outbreak of war had been made redundant – so in February 1940, in desperation, he joined the army. He was aged 37. At the end of April he was shipped, without even a gun, to France to join the collapsing British Expeditionary Force.

What were they thinking of?

In the chaos, he lost contact with his unit, was captured and spent five years as a prisoner of war in Poland. The War Office decided in May 1940 without any reason, that he must have deserted and immediately stopped his wages. I think anyone, let alone my maternal grandmother, might have had a nervous breakdown in that situation. Months later his real status was recognised and his money restored.

My grandfather never talked about his experiences in Poland until I sat him down in 1983 and taped his recollections. He had been greeted on his repatriation with the accusation that he had been lucky and had no idea how bad the war had been, and so he kept quiet. No-one in the family knew, for example, that he was one of the prisoners taken on the 1944-45 death march to Austria by the Germans escaping the Russians in that bitterly cold winter, when so many of his fellow prisoners died or were shot. He was sitting in a field in Austria, with the German guards gone, when an American platoon liberated him and his fellow survivors. He said to me that some of the men went wild with joy, several even trying to ride a horse bare back.

I asked him about escaping and the sort of jolly japes that were portrayed in the prisoner of war camps for officers. He told me it was absolutely nothing like that because he had to work – at one time in a salt mine.

And escaping?

As he said – where would he have gone? There was barbed wire and guards but he said that they weren't really locked down as the Germans knew they wouldn't know what to do if they ran away. He was told that London was being bombed and that Britain was losing the war – but he frankly didn't believe either statement as he couldn't imagine such brutality.

My father was evacuated from London to a farming family in Williton, Somerset, which he found a great relief until at the age of 14 – school leaving age – his mother summoned him back to start working for W H Smith. His father was a bus driver, which in the 30s was a highly valued steady job, but many of his relatives were in the printing trade which is how he got that job.

On my paternal grandmother's side there were some really rum and colourful characters. Her mother, my great grandmother, known as grandma, had lost her husband, John Bright, in a collision on the Thames. He had been, I think, a barge ship's captain. Although my great grandfather was a teetotaller, the subsequent enquiry squarely blamed him for being drunk at the time – for which there was not a shred of evidence.

Grandma was apparently not daunted – and managed to have a further two children, including Aunty May, with a man who was never talked about. The shame of illegitimacy was always something that Aunty May and her full brother, Uncle Stan, felt deeply. Grandma's boys seemed to have a knack for marrying women whose name rhymed with theirs – so we had Horace and Doris and Stan and Nan – while May's husband, (Great) Uncle Fred, who was a lovely man, had been a deserter at some point and used to have real problems every time the doorbell went because he thought it was the military police. Eventually they did come for him.

Fred's parents were killed by a V2 direct hit on their house – and that was really the only war story I heard from my relatives until I taped my grandfather.

My fondest picture of May and Fred remains when May got stuck in a bath, made slippery with bath oil. Uncle Fred, about half her size – imagine a McGill postcard – tried to pull her out, but it was so slippery he ended up in the bath with her. When they eventually managed to get help, even the fire brigade found it very difficult to get them both out of the oily bath – and very embarrassing.

Up until I was born my mother was a nursery nurse and after that she never had a paid job. Her thwarted intelligence really ate away at her and she was hard on everyone – including herself. When I was living on my own in my teens I occasionally, but as rarely as possible, would go home – I called it that but I never really lived in Diss – and each time I had 36 hours of absolute, unbelievable hell at her hands, as she verbally abused me, culminating at least one time in her saying venomously, "And you needn't think I'm proud of you."

Each time I went *home*, I always forlornly hoped that someone might be pleased to see me.

Very occasionally, later, I would talk to her seriously and if I could get her attention she would really try to use her intelligence to understand concepts – she was briefly fascinated, for example, by *transactional analysis*, and the idea that we adopt different personae when dealing with different situations.

I'm not sure she ever really understood that parenting could also have a nurturing side. For me any serious conversation with her was a brief glimpse into a dark and twisted world of thwarted promise.

My father, when I was first conscious of him, worked as a *collector* – so that anyone who ordered an out of stock book in a London Smith's branch could have it later that day – eat your heart out Amazon – as collectors walked to the publisher concerned and picked the book up. He subsequently worked on nights at the old *Daily Herald*, before becoming a rep for the

Daily Telegraph and then *The Times*. In those days the print unions tightly controlled who got a job anywhere in London – and his turn came. For a short period my parents were quite prosperous as the jobs, fully unionised, were well paid.

When they moved to Norfolk – the reason for which I never understood – he had long periods of unemployment and a range of jobs. If nothing else had been, this would have been corrosive. He was a remote figure to me. I remember the only time he hugged me. I was about 18 and he and my mother had had another vicious fight – all words, no physical abuse – and I felt absolutely distraught even though this wasn't uncommon. That hug from him was quite an epoch for me – because at the time it helped and was the only bit of human affection I remember.

I remember a teacher at Bedonwell primary school in Bexleyheath, where my parents moved to from south London, saying to the class, *think about that moment at the end of the day when your mother comes to you and tucks you up in bed and kisses you goodnight.*

I was bewildered.

My mother was deeply ambitious for us. She had little idea of what was possible and no real understanding, but she transferred her longing on to her children. She had a desperate faith in meritocracy but it never made her sympathetic. The worst times were during exams for any of the siblings. She would become distraught and really vicious – a sort of reaction to her own feelings of frustration. My GCE O Levels were the first experience of this in the family – and after my first exam I got home wanting to do revision, only to be forced out to do gardening all afternoon, paradoxically because she was so wound up about my exams.

I was rather upset. No understanding. No affection.

For at least the last three years of her life before she died at 89, my mother suffered from Alzheimer's. It's a pretty dreadful condition of course, but I was comforted that after her lifetime of struggle and angst, she couldn't remember much of the vicissitudes of her life – and for the only time I had known her she was happy – even making jokes about *still being here to annoy everyone*. And I was so pleased.

I know that it is difficult to understand the depths of innocence or ignorance that exist in such a situation. My parents were politically aware enough to tell me about the National Health Service and the other achievements of the Attlee government, but had no real comprehension of how power and privilege worked. I therefore grew up with a vague – there were never many details – but strong sense of injustice and the contempt directed at working class people. I did have examples. There was my maligned paternal great grandfather, unrepresented at the tribunal, my maternal grandfather's experience of the war – during which his mother died and her possessions – some handed down to her and valuable apparently – were spirited away, and the ghastly experience my father had in post-war Berlin.

I absorbed a message that the world was very tough and if you weren't prepared to be tough yourself, you would be trampled on and exploited. No-one said as much, in fact in my recollection no-one said very much at all, but there was a deep atmosphere that I guess made me stubbornly determined – and probably very difficult.

If songs define you at a certain time, it was Paul Simon's *I Am A Rock* that spoke to and for me. I couldn't believe there was another person who felt as I did.

My only real solace was the public library. I was reading three or four books a week. (I remember being told off by the librarian for trying to bring back two books that I had read on the same day I took them out.) I read everything, being frightened beyond my imagination by Kurt Vonnegut's *Sirens of Titan*; bored to death by *Martin Chuzzlewit*; so excited and scared by *Wuthering Heights* that I read it all night, finishing it at 4.00am; rather sickened and put off physicality of any kind, by *An American Dream* which I scarcely understood; loving *What ho, Jeeves!*; being completely baffled by *Kim*; but finding Stan Barstow's *A Kind of Loving* so brilliantly written and generally escaping reality that I longed to be a writer.

I read a mass of non-fiction too and I really was that lonely figure of an autodidact.

No wonder the Tories were so delighted to use austerity to castrate the library service in the UK – ignorance being one of their greatest friends.

The engine of social mobility, as the fantasy had it, came into my life under the misleading title of a meritocracy, and things became far worse.

Grammar School

At the age of 11 I left home – not physically but certainly mentally, socially and intellectually.

I went to a grammar school.

And so began the seven unhappiest years of my life. The brother who was closest to me in age and my best, not to say only, friend became a stranger. My parents had absolutely no comprehension of me and my life. And when I said that I was extremely unhappy on the only occasion when I tried to talk to them – as it happens at the end of the first week at the school – they shook their heads and told me, "*It's a very good school.*"

An experience in those traumatic first weeks taught me the meaning and the importance of *Shibboleth*. And how the binary contrast between *them* and *us* was at the heart of my experience, and, I guess that of other working class children, when I started grammar school.

To begin with, I certainly had no concept of the distinction between *us* and *them* and even if I had done, I wouldn't have had a clue who either *them* or *us* were. Which proved I was one of *them* because those who saw themselves as *us* certainly did know what this distinction was and how important it was and the fact that they were *us*.

Our first Latin homework was the touchstone.

We were sent home with our *Clarendon Latin Course* book with the instruction to do the first exercise on the dative case. No explanation – except an extremely irritated answer to my despairing question: *the indirect object*.

Whether explicit or not, it was a classic example of the way the school sorted the sheep from the goats. (Or those who said **SH**ibboleth and those who said **S**ibboleth.) The sheep were the very bright working class boys from the local council estates – in St Mary Cray, Sidcup, Chelsfield and Orpington – chosen by a highly selective school on the basis of intelligence tests. The goats were the boys from middle class homes in Chislehurst.

And me? I belonged to neither group. Being from out of the area, didn't help one little bit, nor did the nearly 3 hours travelling every day, especially on the erratic 21A bus service.

I was equally baffled by both sheep and goats.

The goats, whose parents knew what the dative was, and whose sons could ask for help and get it, not only did the homework, but were praised for it. The sheep, which included me in this case, hadn't a clue. We were excoriated for not knowing what the dative was and, even more severely, for not having the gumption to find out by asking our parents.

I had asked mine. My father had said, I think with unconscious humour, that it sounded like a different language.

Chislehurst and Sidcup Grammar School for Boys – only boys in those days – was really two schools in one and in real terms wasn't able to cope with the sheep. So many of the sheep – not all but a large number – were frozen out and even though they had been identified as very bright at 11, actually left school at 15, not having taken one public exam.

The school turned successes into failures.

Meritocracy?

I, on the other hand, was just an outsider – completely isolated at home and at school, trying desperately to make friends and tagging along with some sheep out of persistence and unhappiness. I had so little in common with them it was bound to be disastrous – but I felt I had no choice as I had even less in common with the goats.

The teachers mostly didn't notice me and, if they did, it was with what seemed to me to be total indifference and incomprehension and, I later realised, occasional anger as *I was still there.*

By the time of the sixth form, my parents had moved away to Norfolk and I lived on my own – latterly in Sidcup. The teachers knew and talked about it behind my back as I learnt when I took the role of Rosalind in *As You Like It* – but they offered not a crumb of assistance and never even once asked how I was getting on.

In fact the teachers I mainly came into contact with in the Classics department did their best, probably unconsciously, to make life intolerable. As I had taken Greek instead of science up to GCE O Level, I had to do Latin, Greek and Ancient History for A Level. I was outraged as I was desperate to take English and drop Ancient History – few people took 4 A Levels in the '60s.

After a month of constant badgering I was allowed to take English as long as I also took Ancient History. I think they thought I'd give up. Then after the mocks in the term before the actual A Levels they said I could drop Ancient History. It had just been provocation. I nevertheless took the exam having done all the course.

Taking the part of Rosalind was quite a moment for me. It was one achievement at the school when I wasn't made to feel a total failure. Drama wasn't much regarded by the school hierarchy – it certainly wasn't a subject – so my success in the role wasn't a problem to them, but it gave me some confidence in myself, something I remembered in my teaching days, when I put on school productions and my own plays and musicals – and saw so many children grow into themselves.

On the opposite side I had my predicted grades at A Level which in retrospect seem vindictive and seemed so even at the time. It was showing what they thought of me, as if being the only person not made a prefect in my very small upper sixth form of eleven boys, wasn't sign enough.

I'm not doubting for one moment that I was a very awkward and stubborn person who became more and more distressed as the years at school went by. I had no idea at first what was going on in my quotidian world, and by the end of the seven years I really wasn't much wiser, if at all. At the time it seemed to me that there must be a key to this bewildering world and that the other boys, mainly from Chislehurst, knew what it was and guarded the secret well. It felt like a never-ending torture not knowing what was going on, unable to fit the reality to what I was told. It feels to me now that the odds of being able to achieve anything were stacked entirely against me and anyone in a similar position.

We had it dinned into us that *if you work hard, you will get on – and the sky's the limit*. Discovering how much that was a complete hoax took me far longer than it should have done – but as a teenager I had no way of refuting it although I knew first hand that it didn't appear to be true.

The reason, however, there is such a warm, right wing glow about grammar schools is that some less advantaged children did very well and broke out of their class. And as the victors always write the history and have obituaries, it is generally seen that successful people who had benefited from what is actually a sort of social mobility had been to grammar schools and had done well.

So grammar schools are wonderful.

As a bright chap I tried – and my stubbornness meant that I did, as I said earlier, complete my A Levels, go to university and get my Ph.D. The external examiner told me that as far as he was concerned it was one of the most thought-provoking and intellectually important theses that he had read. That didn't, however, appear to count in academic circles. I had sweated blood producing that thesis with a determination to understand important themes in George Eliot's novels, but I still couldn't get the job of university lecturer in English that I was desperate for.

I did get one interview but it turned out I was just a non-threatening make-weight. We started the day of interviews with the professor stating that he didn't think we could appoint as one of the candidates hadn't turned up. Fifteen minutes later, when he did, we could – and it was apparent that he had the job before we started.

I didn't fit their profile – and they didn't know how to deal with me. I was presented with the prevailing orthodoxy that Henry James was the best critic of George Eliot, and I challenged it pointing out that Henry James himself said that he was the worst possible critic because all he did was re-write novels so they were as he would have written them (which he did with *Daniel Deronda* as *The Portrait of a Lady*) and also that he held to the view that her finest novel was *Romola* – which he said was a flawed masterpiece. Just try reading *Romola* and you won't trust James.

The interviewers didn't argue with me although two of them told me that I was wrong.

Years later I was told by the person on the panel who wanted to appoint me that I was by far the best candidate, but because I was unknown – and, worse, knew nobody – they couldn't, or wouldn't, appoint me. So they didn't appoint that day. The other candidate got the job a month later.

Before giving up my ambition totally and joining the IT industry, I kept applying for university jobs. During those nine years I taught very successfully in a secondary modern, a grammar school and two very large – one split site – comprehensives. The grammar school in Thetford was still turning out failures of people who had been successful, as well as its odd successes. The secondary modern, Wymondham School (not Wymondham College) – a really well run and dynamic environment – created some successes out of failures but there was always the feeling amongst the children that they had already failed in life.

The comprehensives were a different experience. Not particularly well run – and that makes a huge difference – they did offer a real opportunity for nearly every pupil. Bloody hard work for the teachers – but so much better for the children. I guess being scarred by my own schooling, it affected how I taught and what I taught. First I went to the Denes High School Lowestoft as a scale 2 teacher, after which I became a *Senior Teacher* and Head of English in a split site comprehensive in Treorchy in the Rhondda Valley, one of the most deprived areas of the UK.

I tried to think from the pupil's point of view – every individual pupil. I don't suppose I succeeded much, but I do know I helped teenagers think for themselves – even when they found that hard – and I used drama to bring out different qualities in people.

I succeeded in uniting the English Department in Treorchy – we were in separate blocks and there were so many rivalries that it had no coherence. Because I was English and had all my character faults, they actually hated me rather more than each other so banded together. It wasn't the most pleasant four years.

When, in some despair and rather deep depression, I left teaching and joined the IT industry, my new colleagues always said that now I would know what real work was like – especially without those long holidays. Initially I tried to tell them that I'd never worked harder – and I certainly haven't – than as an English teacher.

I was so disgusted when the Tories under Theresa May wanted to bring back grammar schools. In fact what they really wanted was to bring back secondary moderns – and we know what that so-called *parity of esteem* between grammar schools and secondary moderns actually means.

Not that the Tories actually use the education system that they think is good enough for the rest of us and which they cheerfully underfund. It took me years to realise that they have their own entirely separate education system. Initially I was always puzzled why I was asked, twenty years later, which school I went to. I soon realised why.

Loving teaching but hating being a teacher in Thatcher's Britain, I wanted to escape the nightmare. I just wanted to write and in 1982 I bought – at hideous and desperate expense, £2,500, when my salary was £15,000 – an Apricot computer and a printer, and was determined to teach myself word processing. In fact the IT system scarcely worked – in those days printing from a PC was something that would happen properly in some distant future. I had all the problems you can imagine.

In 1984 in the Netherlands Philips, a company always ahead of its time in thinking though unable to market itself effectively, had decided that the next generation of computer users wouldn't be computer specialists, so they needed people to write manuals and develop training who were also not computer specialists. I saw an advertisement, applied and for once I absolutely fitted the profile they needed. My salary, for a neophyte with no actual qualifications in IT except the experience of teaching myself word processing, was c£18,000 against the £15,000 I was getting as a highly trained, successful and experienced, very senior teacher.

I did work hard in IT. I did get on and it wasn't so restricting as the public sector, but it still mattered who you knew. And I worked on that harder than the work.

MINO

So far so personal – and highly individual at that. I suppose my message at this point would be that the '60s meritocracy – actually really some sort of development of social mobility – was not entirely illusory but for many working class aspirants more a false concept than a fact.

I know it took a long time for the penny to drop with me and I should have put two and two together much earlier. Countless obituaries have sentences like: *I really didn't know what I would do when I left school or university, but I was introduced by my father to X, who worked for [some prestigious organisation] and he offered me a job – and I never looked back.*

I remember the grandson of the person who wrote what was the standard history of the Ancient Greeks, and whose father was a professor at Cambridge, saying that he had got his lectureship entirely through merit and there was no question of nepotism. I owe him a debt. He forced the scales from my eyes.

In case anyone thinks I still feel bitter about this – I don't. But I do feel bitter about the hypocrisy that keeps on saying *work hard, and you'll get on*, and that it doesn't matter who you or your parents know.

At the same time as the concept of a meritocracy was being developed, there were signs that it wasn't what was actually happening – that it was a meritocracy in name only. For example, in the first stages of the expansion of the universities in the sixties and seventies, there was awareness that the new, large numbers of graduates would not get the jobs that they should expect in a real meritocracy.

The statement that was used to dampen expectations was fascinating. *Just being a graduate doesn't guarantee a job.* The point was well made and accurate – the people who had got the plum jobs before the university expansion happened sometimes to be graduates, but that didn't really matter. Those people were *us*, and in the '60s and '70s they were still the people getting the jobs.

I realised as I approached 30 that I couldn't get the job that I desperately wanted as I knew no-one who mattered, was socially awkward and out of my depth, despite my academic capabilities, and hadn't had the insight to make sure I knew the right people.

So I failed. I realised that I wasn't Will Ladislaw but Tertius Lydgate. (Of course since I never found the key to the meritocracy I was also probably Casaubon.)

A Real Meritocracy?

I think we have to re-assess what a real meritocracy could be, and distinguish it from social mobility, because looking at the individual and the individual's experience is not that useful, even though it is often fascinating, because it is never properly representative.

At an individual level you can counter my experience with many people's different experiences. *Ah yes but X succeeded – so it must be down to you that you didn't.*

I don't doubt that my individual capabilities or lack of them contributed to my failure – but it wasn't the only, and it certainly wasn't the most important, determining factor. And I think the focus on the individual when talking about a meritocracy is the wrong perspective. This isn't an individual thing at all – but a social matter.

We should start our understanding of a meritocracy from the position of what is important and what real success is. I think the pandemic has taught a lot of people that hedge fund managers, offshore billionaires manipulating stock markets and social media to rig elections, internet entrepreneurs and private equity asset strippers bribing people with their own money, have very little merit – and in contrast we know only too well who the people are who do have real merit.

But we also know who takes the lion's share of our resources.

To create a meritocracy we have to ensure that proper rewards go to those who merit our respect.

I do realise the utopian aspects of what I am writing. I just can't bear the current dystopian world.

In my lifetime, we have seen the destruction of any sense among intelligent people that there is a meritocracy and real social mobility – and while I welcome the clarity this is bringing, it seems to me we have created a kakocracy. According to Oxfam, the 8 richest billionaires in the world now have as much wealth as the 3.6 billion people who make up the poorest half of the world's population.

According to the Guardian, the world's richest 26 people own half of the world's wealth.

They are unaccountable to anyone, appear to pay minimal taxes, and manipulate the way we think with impunity. The control of our perception about meritocracy through the billionaire controlled media, confusing it with social mobility, plays into the hands of those who can point to some examples of social mobility.

There is a very tight control in the offshore-owned media of what is politically acceptable. It's often call the *Overton Window*. For example, prior to Thatcher, the idea of selling off our social ownership of the electricity industry to private people was incomprehensible. People like Sir Keith Joseph went full out to make these outrageous ideas seem reasonable, with the efforts funded by untraceable millions.

In my lifetime this *Overton Window* has swung to the far right. I have heard people in pubs saying *we can't afford that as a country*. How brilliant of the rich and powerful to have sold that useful myth so well or convinced people that a national economy is like a household economy. It is no wonder that those rich people spend so much money on false messages, hiding the truth, turning poor people against other poor people. As we have seen with the rise of populism, *deflection* is the propaganda weapon of choice, preferably backed up with ignorance.

I don't know if my personal journey from individual aspiration to awareness of the hollow nature of MINO, and my focus on our collective experience and valuing the right people, is shared. I have to hope it is.

A real meritocracy, however, will have to remove that perception and look at what merits giving people wealth, and then control and power over their lives. Judged by that standard, the last thing we have is a meritocracy.

I always remember that the Black Death started to put the nails into the coffin of feudalism and ushered in the rise of capitalism, which was very progressive in its time. I hope it's not too fanciful to imagine that the current pandemic might have permanent, positive effects on perception and reality and at least stimulate a discussion about a real meritocracy.

BITE-SIZED BOOKS

Bite-Sized Public Affairs Books are designed to provide insights and stimulating ideas that affect us all in, for example, journalism, social policy, education, government and politics.

They are deliberately short, easy to read, and authoritative books written by people who are either on the front line or who are informed observers. They are designed to stimulate discussion, thought and innovation in all areas of public affairs. They are all firmly based on personal experience and direct involvement and engagement.

The most successful people all share an ability to focus on what really matters, keeping things simple and understandable. When we are faced with a new challenge most of us need quick guidance on what matters most, from people who have been there before and who can show us where to start.

They can be read straight through at one easy sitting and then referred to as necessary – a trusted repository of hard-won experience.

BITE-SIZED BOOKS

Catalogue

Bite-Sized Books cover business, public affairs, lifestyle, fiction and children's fiction. The full catalogue can be found at:

https://bite-sizedbooks.com/product-category/all/